— ALEXANDRIA'S — FREEDMEN'S CEMETERY

• *A Legacy of Freedom* •

DISCARD

CHAR McCARGO BAH

Edited by Mumini M. Bah

THE
History
PRESS

Published by The History Press
Charleston, SC
www.historypress.com

Cover images: Artist Mario Chiodo's sculpture *The Path of Thorns and Roses* and sculptor Joanna Blake's *The Memorial's Bas-Reliefs*, with Steven Halperson of Tisara Photography.

First published 2019

Manufactured in the United States

ISBN 9781467140010

Library of Congress Control Number: 2018958988

Notice: The information in this book is true and complete to the best of our knowledge. It is offered without guarantee on the part of the author or The History Press. The author and The History Press disclaim all liability in connection with the use of this book.

CONTENTS

FOREWORD

During the Civil War, Alexandria, Virginia, was quickly occupied by the Union army to prevent the Confederates from entering the United States capital. Many freed and enslaved African Americans poured into the city for protection. Demographic records show that the population of Alexandria grew by several thousand each year. In 1861, by order of General Benjamin Franklin Butler of Fort Monroe in Hampton, Virginia, these men, women and children became "contraband of war," and their labor was used to support the Union cause. As the Civil War progressed, slaves knew that a chance at freedom lay behind the lines of a Union-occupied area. Their arrival in this occupied city gave them a chance at freedom, although many did not live long in freedom.

The original Freedmen's Cemetery was created by the authority of the United States Army in 1864, toward the end of the Civil War. Reverend Albert Gladwin was appointed by the army as superintendent of the Cemetery. It was an answer to the growing humanitarian crisis created by the deaths of many who arrived sick or became ill after their arrival. Many people died in Alexandria before the creation of the Cemetery, and their identities are unknown to us. For more than 1,700 freed and contraband, fate intervened via the army.

In a simple ledger known as the "Gladwin Records," Reverend Gladwin recorded the marriages, births and deaths of the freedmen and contrabands along with other information related to the Cemetery. This ledger, kept after Gladwin's dismissal in 1865, is a remarkable document that was used to connect descendants of the contrabands and the Freedmen's Cemetery.

Char McCargo Bah was the official city genealogist for the Cemetery. Ms. McCargo Bah used the Gladwin Records and her own unique investigational

Audrey P. Davis, director of
Alexandria Black History Museum.
Courtesy Catherine Weinraub.

research to permit us to discover the lives of those buried at the Cemetery between 1864 and 1869. Her research enabled her to identify more than one thousand people who are directly related to those buried at the site. They are the living, breathing legacy of this memorial. Their story is America's history. Their ancestors' Civil War experiences expand our knowledge of the conflict and the growth of Alexandria during Reconstruction. In the aftermath of the war, these families helped to rebuild Alexandria. Their perseverance aided them in the fight against Jim Crow oppression and second-class citizenship. Their stories and the stories of their families after the war attest to the power of faith, hope and determination in the face of horrific persecution.

In 2014, the City of Alexandria held a dedication of the now National Historic Contrabands and Freedmen's Cemetery Memorial that restored honor and dignity to the final resting place of a forgotten people. The joyful occasion was the result of the efforts of many people who worked hard to ensure that this story at this site was never wiped from the memories of Alexandrians again.

The families in this book are fourth, fifth and sixth generations of Alexandria's African American community. In each profile you read, I am sure you will find things that will amaze and inspire you. Like many other American families, these families achieved the American dream. Through forced relocation and unimaginable brutality, they made this country their home and helped to make it great.

Every student should read this book. It will help them to understand the history of this city and the role African Americans played and continue to play in its development. I know readers will gain useful insight from this book and will refer to it often. *Alexandria's Freedmen's Cemetery: A Legacy of Freedom* is an African American history of Alexandria, Virginia, during the Civil War and its aftermath. By purchasing and reading this book, you will keep Alexandria's freedmen and contrabands a living, breathing people.

Audrey P. Davis,
Director, Alexandria Black History Museum,
Alexandria, Virginia,
July 1, 2018

FOREWORD

I first met Char McCargo Bah when I was researching my family. I was curious about whether my family had ancestors buried at the Contrabands and Freedmen's Cemetery. As a child, I knew the site was a gas station. It made me very uncomfortable, and I could not explain why. Although I was not able to help Char with my family history, she discovered that three of my ancestors were buried at the Cemetery—three had been unknown to my family.

In September 2014, the Cemetery Memorial was dedicated on a weekend called "Journey to Be Free." The Descendants' Banquet prior to the dedication included Char speaking for the ancestors. In that speech, she said that the ancestors were surprised that the descendants were present to recognize them. In their minds, they felt that the desecration and disrepair of the site over the years meant that they have been forgotten, that part of their arduous journey to freedom had been in vain. This book and her words spoken were for all those buried in that place, and it is our opportunity and yours to experience that journey. The actual dedication ceremony was a long-overdue memorial service, and it was our chance to give honor to those whose lives had been so unimaginably difficult.

This book further connects those descendants Char identified to their ancestors by revealing little-known or unknown information regarding their ancestors' lives. She provides the reader with research tools and use of census data, marriage licenses, death records, tax records and city directories, among other things she so tirelessly utilized to obtain information. She uncovered those whose lives were partially—and, in some cases, deliberately—erased, and she restored them to their rightful place in their families and in history.

With what I now know, my life will never be the same. I have a greater sense of wholeness, and while I don't know yet my place in the diaspora, I feel like I have a place of origin. That history does not become history until we make it ours. I give Char McCargo Bah all the credit for what I know today. As I have gotten to know my family, I can now better understand my determination. I know where my deep faith comes from, and I know where my strength lies. In the narratives in this book, I see that the ancestors carved out better lives for themselves after the Civil War. Their successes propelled us to our accomplishments. The disturbing message I was receiving regarding the gas station site is gone and is now replaced with recognition. As for my relationship with Char, I have gained a dear friend who feels very much like a part of my family.

This work is important to the descendants. We share being descendants, but our stories are different. It is also important to anyone trying to understand this awful time in the history of the city of Alexandria and the nation. The narratives regarding those previously unknown are filled with struggle and suffering but also resilience. The insights into lives after freedom are remarkable. This is a must-read for those with an interest in ancestry and genealogy. For those with an interest in the Civil War era who want a glimpse into lives after the war, this book is important.

We must never forget those who died and all they contributed.

FRANCES NORTON BURTON,
Freedmen's Cemetery Descendant,
July 1, 2018

ACKNOWLEDGEMENTS

B ack in 2008, when the City of Alexandria asked me to work on the Freedmen's Cemetery Descendants' project, I knew then that this story had to be told. Along the way, there were many people and institutions that played a role in the Freedmen's Cemetery. I particularly wish to acknowledge former congressman James (Jim) Moran Jr., current Alexandria mayor Allison Silberberg, former mayor William D. Euille, City Manager Mark Jinks, former director J. Lance Mallamo of the Office of Historic Alexandria and his former assistant, Robin J. Moscati, and former Alexandria Public Information Officer Amy Bertsch and Communications Officer Andrea Blackford for their expertise on the Freedmen's Cemetery project.

The Alexandria Black History Museum (ABHM) staff was instrumental in providing assistance, support, programming and meeting space for the Freedmen's Cemetery Descendants' events. Those who provided their services included Director Audrey P. Davis and her staffers, Jewel Plummer, Melissa Hand Leathers, Dennis Doster and Lillian S. Patterson.

The Office of Historic Alexandria Department, Archaeology Division, worked tirelessly to reclaim the Freedmen's Cemetery and participated in planning the Freedmen's Cemetery and the Descendants' events. Special acknowledgements go to Dr. Pamela J. Cressey, former city archaeologist; Francine Bromberg, former city archaeologist; Ruth Reeder, former education coordinator of archaeology; and Annie Lynch (deceased) and Alissa Schrider, former volunteers. Others who provided their expertise included Katy Cannady, Marilyn Patterson, Shelia Whiting, Cheryl Lawrence and Cheryl Anne Colton.

This project would not have been possible if it were not for two private citizens who founded the Friends of Freedmen's Cemetery in 1997. The founders were Lillie Finklea and Louise Massoud, and their volunteer board members included Tim Dennee, Char McCargo Bah, Shellyn McCaffrey and Ludwig Gaines.

The Alexandria Library of Local History/Special Collections' staff provided support throughout the research process of this book. Special thanks to former branch manager George Combs, reference librarian Leslie Anderson, former media librarian Julia Downie and librarian assistant Mark Zoeter.

Special thanks go to Selma Stewart, former president of the Afro-American Historical and Genealogical Society of Hampton Roads Chapter and a board member of the Virginia Genealogical Society, who provided the author with a little-unknown history of Alexandria, Virginia, during the Civil War.

The majority of the photographs in this book were taken by Steven Halperson of Tisara Photography in Alexandria, Virginia. Thank you, Steven.

Without the descendants, this project would not have existed. The descendants' willingness to participate in the research process made it possible for the author to connect them to the Freedmen's Cemetery. A warm thank-you goes out to all these descendants.

Finally, my friends and family have supported me throughout this journey by providing support, editing, brainstorming sessions, traveling partners and mentorship. Thanks to my husband, Mumini M. Bah; daughter, Maimoona N. Bah Duckenfield; mother, Bernice V. McCargo; brothers, Jasper Lee McCargo Jr. and Bernard McCargo; sister, Shirley Mae McCargo Turner; cousin Deborah A. Abbott, PhD; and my friends Damita Drayton Green, Michelle Todd, Brenda Nelson, Tawana C. Thomas, Nathania A. Branch Miles, Frances Burton Norton, Carolyn Phillips McCrae, Norma Jennings Turner and Charlene Taylor Napper.

There will be omissions, failings and shortcomings in this project, but I have strived to do my best to identify the descendants of the Freedmen's Cemetery. I hope that readers will communicate to me whether there are other potential descendants of the Freedmen's Cemetery (you can contact me at findingthingsforu@gmail.com).

CONTRIBUTORS

Joyce Paige Anderson Abney is a native Alexandrian. After working for thirty-five years, she retired from the Washington, D.C., Public School System. She attended Lyles-Crouch Elementary School and Parker-Gray High School in Alexandria. In 1977, she graduated from Cardozo Adult School in Washington, D.C. Prior to moving to Washington, D.C., she was a member of Alfred Street Baptist Church in Alexandria.

Lillian Locklear Alston is a native Baltimorean. She is a retired assistant principal, having spent her career in the Baltimore City Public School System. In 1962, she became a social studies teacher, and in 1972, she became an assistant principal. In 1955, she graduated from Frederick Douglass High School. Her Gaines relatives were early members of Shiloh Baptist Church in Alexandria.

Judy Patricia Coles Bailey, MD, was born in Harlem Hospital in New York City. She is a doctor of internal medicine and a part-time educator. In 1960, she graduated from Carver High School in Spartanburg, South Carolina. Her Armstead and Jackson relatives were early members of Third Baptist Church and Ebenezer Baptist Church in Alexandria.

Dena Banks is a native Alexandrian. Dena and her husband, Garold Mobley, are entrepreneurs. They own Mosaic Barber and Beauty Salons in Dumfries, Virginia. Dena also retired from the Prince William County Public School System. In 1979, she graduated from Woodbridge Senior High School in Woodbridge, Virginia. Her Arrington and Simms relatives were nineteenth-century members of Alfred Street Baptist Church in Alexandria.

Reverend Ronald Eugene Burke Sr. was born in New York to native Alexandrians. He served as a Baptist minister for forty years prior to retirement. He spent twenty years as a civil rights activist with the Southern Christian Leadership Conference and with the Operation PUSH (People United to Save Humanity) in Illinois. In 1952, Mr. Burke graduated from Commerce High School in New York City. Since the nineteenth century, his Burke family have held membership in Alfred Street Baptist Church in Alexandria.

Frances Norton Burton is a native Alexandrian. She has been appointed by the California State Senate to serve a third term as a public member of the Dental Board of California. She attended Charles Houston Elementary School. In 1962, she graduated from Calvin Coolidge High School in Washington, D.C. Since the nineteenth century, her Robinson and Carter relatives have held membership at Roberts Memorial United Methodist Church in Alexandria. Her Norton family are members of Shiloh Baptist Church.

Lynnwood Campbell is a native Alexandrian. He is a retired certified public accountant. In 1960, Lynwood was the first African American to attend St. Mary's Elementary School in Alexandria. He also attended St. Joseph's Catholic Elementary School. In 1965, he graduated from Western High School in Washington, D.C. Lynwood is a lifetime member of St. Joseph's Catholic Church in Alexandria.

Lawrence Oliver Carter is a native Alexandrian. After thirty-eight years of service, he retired from the Library of Congress as an automated operations coordinator. He attended St. Joseph's Catholic Elementary School. In 1965, he graduated from Parker-Gray High School in Alexandria. Mr. Carter is a member and usher at St. Mary's Catholic Church of Piscataway in Clinton, Maryland.

Lois Diggs Davis is a native Alexandrian. She is a retired director of corporate sponsorship and conventions of the National Community Pharmacist Association in Alexandria, Virginia. She attended Seminary School and Lyles-Crouch Elementary School. In 1959, she graduated from Parker-Gray High School. She is a member of Oakland Baptist Church in Alexandria.

Richard Diggs is a native Alexandrian. He is president and CEO of Alexandria Pest Services in Springfield, Virginia. He attended Charles Houston Elementary School, Parker-Gray High School and George Washington High School. In 1972, he graduated from T.C. Williams High School in Alexandria. He is a member of Woodlawn Faith United Methodist Church in Alexandria.

Howard Dishman is a native Alexandrian. He retired with thirty-five years of service as a manager for a dry cleaning business. His wife, Dana, retired as a case manager for Alexandria Mental Health Services. Mr. Dishman was educated in Alexandria and Washington, D.C., School Systems. They are active members of Meade Memorial Episcopal Church in Alexandria.

Eugene S. Drayton is a native Alexandrian. He is a retired law librarian for the Los Angeles County Counsel. Eugene attended Charles Houston Elementary School in Alexandria. In 1957, he graduated from Parker-Gray High School. The Drayton family are members of Ebenezer Baptist Church in Alexandria.

Elizabeth Goods Brooks Evans is a native Alexandrian. She retired as a supervisor of consumer services in Washington, D.C. In 1954, Elizabeth graduated from St. Joseph's Catholic Elementary School, and in 1957, she graduated from St. Mary's Academy for Girls in Alexandria. Her relatives are members of St. Joseph's Catholic Church and at Roberts Memorial United Methodist Church in Alexandria.

Gwen Day Fuller is a native Alexandrian. In 2006, she retired from the Newton Massachusetts Public School System. In 1958, she graduated from St. Joseph's Catholic Elementary School, and in 1962, she graduated from St. Mary's Academy in Alexandria. She is a member of St. Joseph's Catholic Church.

Rita Murphy Harris is a native Alexandrian. With thirty-five years of service as a human resource specialist, she retired from the United States Postal Service. She graduated from St. Joseph's Catholic Elementary School in 1961, and she graduated from Parker-Gray High School in 1964. Rita's father was a member of St. Joseph's Catholic Church in Alexandria.

Sherrin Hamilton Bell is a native Philadelphian. She retired as a personnel analyst from the Commonwealth of Pennsylvania. In 1965, Sherrin graduated from Overbrook High School in Philadelphia, Pennsylvania. She was a former member of the Annunciation Episcopal Church in Philadelphia. Currently, she is a member of Pin Memorial Baptist Church in Philadelphia. In the nineteenth century, her Franklin relatives were members of Roberts Memorial United Methodist Church in Alexandria.

Gwen Brown Henderson is a native Alexandrian. She retired from the federal government with forty-one years of service. Gwen attended Lyles-Crouch Elementary School and Parker-Gray Middle School. In 1968, she graduated from T.C. Williams High School. She is a member of Ebenezer Baptist Church in Alexandria.

James E. Henson Sr., Esq., is a native Alexandrian. He is a retired attorney who worked in Howard County, Maryland. He was the first African American attorney to serve as assistant county solicitor in Howard County. In 1954, he graduated from Parker-Gray High School in Alexandria. Mr. Henson has been a member of St. Joseph's Catholic Church in Alexandria since 1937.

Gloria Tancil Holmes is native Alexandrian. She grew up in Fairfax, Virginia. She was a retired Head Start education coordinator. In 1962, she graduated from Parker-Gray High School. Prior to her death in 2016, she was a member of Meade Memorial Episcopal Church in Alexandria.

Doris (Dottie) Williams Hughes is a native Alexandrian. She is a retired professional babysitter. She attended St. Joseph's Catholic School, Lyles-Crouch Elementary School and Parker-Gray High School. Ms. Hughes has been a member of St. Joseph's Catholic Church in Alexandria for more than eighty-six years.

Andrew Johnson is native North Carolinian. He attended elementary school at Our Lady of the Miraculous Medal Catholic School. In 1960, he graduated from Dudley High School. His father was a member of St. Joseph's Catholic Church in Alexandria.

Bernice Robinson Lee is a native Alexandrian. She retired as a primary school teacher in Chicago, Illinois. In 1944, she graduated from Parker-Gray High School. Since the nineteenth century, her Lumpkins relatives have been members at Roberts Memorial United Methodist Church in Alexandria.

Yvette Taylor Lewis is a native Alexandrian. In 2008, she retired as a principal at Hayfield Secondary School in Fairfax County, Virginia. In 1972, she graduated from T.C. Williams High School in Alexandria. Yvette is a member of Ebenezer AME Church in Fort Washington, Maryland. Her Taylor family are members of Third Baptist Church in Alexandria.

James Lightfoot and his sister, Antoinette Lightfoot Jones, are native Alexandrians. James retired as a senior business analyst. James and his sister attended St. Joseph's Catholic School. In 1965, he graduated from Parker-Gray High. The Lightfoot family are members of St. Joseph's Catholic Church in Alexandria.

ZSun-nee (Zunny) Kimball Miller Matema was born in Washington, D.C. She has had a long career as an entrepreneur, educator, actress, artist and writer. She attended St. Augustine Catholic School. In 1961, she graduated from McKinley Technology High School (formerly McKinley Technical High School) in Washington, D.C. Her ancestor Reverend Robert H. Robinson was a nineteenth-century minister at Roberts Memorial United Methodist Church in Alexandria.

Carolyn Phillips McCrae is a native Alexandrian. In 2003, she retired from the U.S. Department of the Navy with forty-one years of outstanding government service. She attended Lyles-Crouch Elementary School. In 1957, she graduated from Parker-Gray High School. Mrs. McCrae continues her family's two-hundred-year legacy as a member of Roberts Memorial United Methodist Church and its predecessor church, Trinity United Methodist in Alexandria.

Betty Dogan Roberts Nicholas is a native Alexandrian. She is a retired government contract "Think Tank" security officer. She attended the original Lyles-Crouch Elementary School. In 1951, she graduated from Parker-Gray High School. She is a member of St. Joseph's Catholic Church in Alexandria.

Lillian Stanton Patterson is a native Alexandrian. She is a retired employee of the City of Alexandria, for whom she was a curator of the Alexandria Black History Museum. In 1944, she graduated from Parker-Gray High School. She is a member and historian for Shiloh Baptist Church in Alexandria. Her Bannon and Currier relatives were early nineteenth-century members of Shiloh Baptist Church.

Fayrene Lyles Richardson is a native Alexandrian. She is a retired federal government employee. In 1961, she graduated from Luther Jackson High School in Merrifield, Virginia. At a young age, she was a member of Woodlawn United Methodist Church. She is currently a member of Fort Washington Baptist Church in Fort Washington, Maryland.

Samuel (Sammie) Shanklin was born in Washington, D.C., at the Freedmen Hospital to native Alexandrians. In 2016, he retired as a security driver for the secretary of the Department of Agriculture, with forty-eight years of service for the federal government and two years of service in the military. Samuel attended Lyles-Crouch Elementary School in Alexandria. In 1965, he graduated from Parker-Gray High School. He is a third-generation member of Roberts Memorial United Methodist Church in Alexandria.

Shirley Sanders Steele is a native Alexandrian. In 2001, she retired with more than twenty-four years of service with Verizon Telecommunication Company. Mrs. Sanders Steele was educated at Parker-Gray High School. In 1977, she graduated from T.C. Williams Adult Night School. She is a member of Community Praise Seventh-day Adventist Church in Alexandria.

Karen Hubbard Suggs is a native Alexandrian. She is an employee of Alexandria City Public School System with more than thirty years of service. Karen attended the Alexandria City Public Schools. In 1975, she graduated from T.C. Williams High School. She is a member of Roberts Memorial United Methodist Church in Alexandria.

John Taylor and Beatrice Cross Taylor are native Alexandrians. In 1996, Mr. Taylor retired from the Washington Metropolitan Area Transit Authority with thirty-four years of service. His wife, Beatrice, also retired in 1996 from the federal government. In 1954, they graduated from Parker-Gray High School. Mrs. Taylor is an active member of Roberts Memorial United Methodist Church in Alexandria, and Mr. Taylor is member of Third Baptist Church in Alexandria.

Frances Colbert Clements Terrell is a native Alexandrian. She is a retired federal government employee who spent twenty-three of her thirty years as Congressional staffer at the United States House of Representatives. Mrs. Terrell attended Lyles-Crouch Elementary School. In 1961, she graduated from Parker-Gray High School. She is a member of Oakland Baptist Church in Alexandria.

Karen Ambush Thande is a native of Massachusetts. She is a retired educator who taught in the Boston Public Schools and the International School of Kenya in East Africa. In 1961, she graduated from South High School in Worcester, Massachusetts. Her Welford and Thornton relatives were members of Roberts Memorial United Methodist Church and Alfred Street Baptist Church in Alexandria.

Eugene R. Thompson is a native Alexandrian. He is a public art and museum management consultant. He was the first director of the Alexandria Black History Resource Center (now Alexandria Black History Museum). His elementary school years were at Lyles-Crouch Elementary School. In 1963, he graduated from Parker-Gray High School. He is a member of Roberts Memorial United Methodist Church in Alexandria.

Norma Jennings Turner was born in Washington, D.C., to native Alexandrians. In 1988, she retired with thirty-nine years of service from the Department of the Army. In 1947, she graduated from Parker-Gray High School. Mrs. Turner has been a member of Roberts Memorial United Methodist Church in Alexandria for more than seventy-five years.

Paula Regina Haskins Williams was a native Alexandrian. Prior to her death on April 7, 2009, she worked for the City of Alexandria's Social Services Department. She attended schools in the Alexandria Public School System, including George Washington High School. She was a member of Oakland Baptist Church in Alexandria.

Gerald Wanzer is a native Alexandrian. He retired as a firefighter for the Alexandria Fire Department. He attended Lyles-Crouch Elementary School. In 1962, he graduated from Parker-Gray High School. His family are members of Oakland Baptist Church in Alexandria.

Adrienne Terrell Washington is a native Alexandrian. She is an award-winning Washington, D.C.–based journalist, television and radio commentator as well as a college professor. In 1968, she graduated from T.C. Williams High School. She is a member at both parent churches Oakland Baptist Church and Meade Memorial Episcopal Church in Alexandria.

INTRODUCTION

The Freedmen's Cemetery was established to accommodate the large number of contrabands and freedmen who died in Alexandria. An influx of slaves coming to Alexandria during the Civil War caused a population explosion. To protect those slaves from their former masters, Alexandria adopted the name "contraband of war," which was first used by General Benjamin Franklin Butler of Fort Monroe in Hampton, Virginia. As they attained the status of "contraband," the former slaves were protected by the Union and could not be returned to their masters.

Many of the contrabands were malnourished and sick when they arrived in Alexandria. Their death toll was high. In 1864, the Federal government seized property at the corner of South Washington and Church Streets to establish a burial ground for the contrabands and freedmen. From 1864 to 1869, more than 1,700 contrabands and freedmen were buried in that cemetery.

After the Civil War, the Cemetery went through several ownerships, the last owner building an office building and a gas station on the Cemetery's property. For more than fifty years, people drove to that gas station without knowing that there were human remains underneath its grounds. Then, in the 1990s, the Woodrow Wilson Bridge Improvement Construction Project involved the gas station and the office building where the Cemetery was located. The city purchased the gas station, and demolition began on the Cemetery property. The demolition exposed human remains, and the Cemetery was rediscovered.

Louise Massoud and Lillie Finklea, activists and Cemetery preservationists. *Courtesy Tisara Photography.*

After its rediscovery, the Archaeology Division confirmed that there were graves on the property. A citizens' group was formed by two residents of Alexandria, Lillie Finklea and Louise Massoud. They were the founders of the Friends of the Freedmen's Cemetery. The group was made up of a volunteer board of directors: Tim Dennee, Char McCargo Bah, Shellyn McCaffrey and Ludwig Gaines. The Friends of the Freedmen's Cemetery and the City of Alexandria started planning for the future of the Cemetery. The project first needed to secure some funds. The city, along with the Woodrow Wilson Bridge Improvement Project and Congressman James Moran Jr., obtained funding for the Freedmen's Cemetery Memorial Park. Once secured, the planning of the Cemetery and locating the descendants of those buried at the Cemetery could begin.

In 2008, the Office of Historic Alexandria Archaeology Department and the Alexandria Black History Museum searched for a genealogist to work on the Freedmen's Cemetery Project. That project was assigned to the author to locate descendants of the Freedmen's Cemetery. The author met with the City of Alexandria to discuss the research plan in locating descendants, including Lance Mallamo, director of the Office of Historic Alexandria; City Archaeologist Dr. Pamela J. Cressey; Amy Bertsch, research historian of the Office of Historic Alexandria; Audrey P. Davis, assistant director of Alexandria Black History Museum; and Dave Cavanaugh of the Alexandria Archaeological Commission. In that meeting, they discussed Gladwin's ledger book. The genealogist made the group aware of a book that author Wesley Pippenger had compiled from the ledger book. Reverend Albert Gladwin was superintendent of contrabands, and he was in charge of the contrabands and freedmen's burials. His records of those burials were very helpful to the genealogist in locating descendants.

From 2008 until 2017, the author located 171 deceased individuals' descendants. The research only covered a certain period. Many of the families in this book were only researched going back to the 1860s, and only a few of the families the author researched went beyond this period; contemporaneous historical events were also included. Those historical findings were included in the book as the "Spoken Words."

Each chapter in this book starts with the Spoken Words, which were written to bring the reader closer to the understanding of the struggle the ancestors faced to obtain their freedom. By researching and reading more than two thousand newspaper articles and books on slavery, the genealogist was moved by the voices of those people who endured bondage.

For the descendants who were found and reconnected to their ancestors, this is just a small window to their history. It is a history of pain and joy, of courage and endurance. It is hoped this book will inspire the descendants and others like them to research their families in order for people to place them in the proper historical context where they belong.

Chapter 1

WE WERE WAITING
ON FREEDOM

It was in the year of 1861 when the Yankees came into Alexandria. We have been hearing about the Civil War and what it could do to our freedom. We freed Negroes were afraid, but when we saw those Union soldiers in blue come riding into Alexandria to protect the area from the Grays, we stood and saluted them with tears running down our cheeks. We shouted out, "Ole Abe!" Yes, our president, Abraham Lincoln, had sent the Union to protect us from the Confederate Grays.

Yes, we were waiting on freedom. Every man, woman, child born freed or enslaved was waiting for freedom for all.

Together, we freed and enslaved Negroes became useful by offering our skills on every job that was needed, for the cause of the war. We worked in the stables, grooming, feeding and shoeing the horses. We helped build the forts to keep the Grays out. We worked at the docks; women cooked, washed clothes and took care of the sick and the babies. We were afraid if Ole Abe's army did not win, we will be in slavery like so many of our enslaved people. But at night, we gathered together and listened and waited to hear about freedom. Yes, we were waiting for freedom.

There were a lot of hope but also a lot of despair. We saw other poor Negroes who had run away from their masters with rags hanging on their skeletal bodies and their bones protruding through their skin. They were near death by the time they got to Alexandria, but they had hope that this time they were going to be freed. As they entered Alexandria, the Union soldiers addressed them as contrabands of war, their status was no longer as slaves. Yes, we all were waiting for freedom.

We knew freedom was coming this time. Several times a day, a new group of Negroes running from their masters entered Alexandria. When they crossed the barricade in Alexandria that we had set up to keep the Confederates out, the enslaved Negroes would collapse on the brown dusty dirty ground and would get up and thank God that they were free behind the Union's barricade. Yes, we were waiting for freedom.

Whether we were freed or enslaved, we were marked by the color of our skin. We all stayed close to the Union soldiers, and we all were waiting for freedom.

Before the Civil War, Alexandria had many freed Negroes; some had purchased their freedom, and others were emancipated by their owners. But with this war, we were all waiting for freedom.

The Civil War put the freed and contrabands together. We worked beside one another and died beside one another. We collected our food and clothes rations, and we prayed together. We were waiting to hear about freedom.

We freed Negroes were known as free people of color. Our surnames told our story. We were the Baltimore, Beckley, Dorsey, Franklin, Gaines, Murphy and Spriggs families. But during the Civil War, we freed Negroes appreciated the faith and hard work of the contrabands who were slaves protected by the Union soldiers. The contrabands came here with nothing but their faith and hope that freedom was coming. So we joined hands with the Brent, Brooks, Brown, Butlers, Gibson, Johnsons and Payne families, and we all were praying and waiting for freedom.

Death was all around us. We all knew when someone died. We heard the mothers singing:

Swing Low, Sweet Chariot
Swing Low, Sweet Chariot,
Comin' for to carry me home!
I looked over Jordan and what did I see,
Comin' for to carry me home....!

Many of the contrabands did not know whether they would see freedom in heaven or freedom on earth. We were just waiting for Freedom.

Children were born one minute and died the next. Old men and old women just could not hang on to see freedom on earth, so they gave up and knew they will be free in heaven. As we waited to hear Ole President Lincoln tell us we were free, we heard the song again: "Swing Low, Sweet Chariot." Another person died and claimed their freedom. For the rest of us, we are "Waiting for Freedom!"

Rita Murphy Harris

Murphy, Rachel—buried September 30, 1865, age five
Butler, Joseph—buried October 16, 1865, age sixty

When Rachel died in September 1865, the weather was unusually sultry with temperatures that felt like July and August. For Rachel's mother, finding transportation for her child's body to be carried to the Cemetery during this hot weather added to her grief for the loss of her child. On October 16, 1865, death claimed Joseph. The two deaths were just two weeks apart, and for each funeral, the weather was different.

The research to find an unknown descendant for Rachel Murphy began with her death date. The genealogist used the 1870 census to identify all African Americans in Alexandria, Virginia, with the surname Murphy. There were only two separate households that had adult females with the last name Murphy; one was Mary Murphy, who was sixty years old, and the other was Mahala Murphy, who was twenty-seven years old (based on other documentation, she may have been older). In order to eliminate one of the Murphy women for Rachel's mother, the researcher focused on Mahala, who was younger than Mary; records that were available during the Civil War were applied to research Mahala. The researcher also used the Freedmen's Bureau Records to locate Mahala, who was in Alexandria during the Civil War. She received housing assistance through the Freedmen's Bureau. Her rent was one dollar, which increased to two dollars for a place at Sickel Barracks in Alexandria.

During the Civil War, numerous contrabands flooded Alexandria. As they came to Alexandria, others were dying from diseases and malnutrition. Mahala carried a heavy burden during the Civil War. She lost her daughter and her brother-in-law at the end of the war. Her husband, John Murphy, was just returning from serving in the United States Colored Troops.

The censuses from 1870 through 1900 revealed that Mahala had ten children, but only four made it to adulthood. Joseph Butler was identified as an indirect relative of Mahala during the research process to connect Rachel to Mahala. Mahala's older children had mentioned their father's name on their marriage licenses as well as their death certificates, which included both parents' names. Eli Butler was Mahala's first husband. Through that research, the researcher discovered that Joseph Butler was the brother-in-law of Mahala.

Travis Murphy (1861–1928). *Courtesy Rita Murphy Harris.*

By using a number of nineteenth- and twentieth-century records, the genealogist found the descendants of Rachel Murphy and Joseph Butler. Based on Mahala's headstone, she was born in 1836. She and her first husband, Eli Butler, had several children in Fauquier, Virginia. Prior to 1860, she met John Murphy, and they became husband and wife. It appears that Mahala was enslaved, which accounts for her not having a marriage license. John was a freed person appearing on the 1850 census in Prince William County, Virginia. John and Mahala migrated to Alexandria, Virginia, with Mahala's three children— Edwin Butler, Ester (Hester) Butler and Scot Butler—sometime between 1860 and 1861. Mahala and John added another child to their family in 1861, Travis, a son born in Alexandria. During the Civil War, John enlisted in the United States Colored Troops, and Mahala stayed in Alexandria, where John's sister was living and Mahala's first husband's family were also living.

By 1870, John, Mahala and their children were living in Alexandria. The last time that Mahala and John appeared on the census as a couple was 1900. In order to locate John and Mahala's descendants, the genealogist researched their children from the nineteenth century through the twentieth-first century. A living descendant connected to John and Mahala's son Travis. Travis married his second wife, Rose Evans Murphy from Fauquier, Virginia, in 1904. They had one child, a son, Elrich William Murphy. Elrich married Marie Elizabeth Henry in 1945, and they had one child, a daughter, Rita Murphy.

After the death of John and Mahala, their son Travis inherited his parents' Alexandria home at 929 North Alfred Street. Travis's son, Elrich was a devout Catholic at St. Joseph's Catholic Church in Alexandria. He worked for sixty-two years as a buyer of religious merchandise. Elrich was a well-known African American photographer in Alexandria, Virginia. On March 31, 1993, Elrich died in New Jersey, his daughter, Rita, by his side.

Rita is the living descendant of Rachel Murphy, and she is the indirect descendant of Joseph Butler at the Alexandria Contrabands and Freedmen's

Rose Evans Murphy and son Elrich W. Murphy (1912). *Courtesy Rita Murphy Harris.*

Rita Murphy Harris and her dad, Elrich W. Murphy. *Courtesy Rita Murphy Harris.*

Cemetery. She never knew that her family members were buried at the Cemetery. Rita and her father were only children. Both of them were raised in the Catholic faith. Her great-grandparents John and Mahala laid a strong foundation of faith, property ownership and hard work that continued to their great-grandchild. Rita has continued that family legacy of hard work, strong faith, family values and work ethnics.

Rita graduated from St. Joseph's Catholic Elementary School and then graduated from Parker-Gray High School in 1964. She pursued further education in business communication and accounting. After she graduated from high school, she married Dale F. Harris. One year later, they had a son, Dale Jr. Rita landed a job with the United States Postal Service. Later, they migrated to New Jersey, where Rita continued to work for the Postal Service. She advanced her career from executive secretary to human resource specialist. After thirty-five years of service, she retired. In her retirement, she became an active volunteer with the Middlesex County Court in New Jersey for Children's Placement Unit resolving family issues. After a number of years of living in New Jersey, Rita and Dale moved to Delaware. On July 19, 2017, Rita lost her husband, Dale.

Dale Jr. followed in his mother's footstep and became an employee at the United States Postal Service. His career accelerated to supervisor for the Consumer Call Center Department in New Jersey.

The genealogist also researched Mahala's children by her first marriage. It revealed that they migrated to Prince William, Virginia; New Jersey; and

Dale Harris Sr. and Dale Harris Jr. *Courtesy Rita Murphy Harris.*

Pennsylvania. Mahala's daughter Ester married Lewis Primas in Alexandria on September 4, 1877. Locating Hester Butler Primas was an important piece of locating the actual death date of Mahala. Ester and Lewis migrated to Prince William, purchased some land, raised their children and at the end of their lives were buried at the Primas Family Cemetery. At the Cemetery are the grave of Mahala Murphy, who died in 1906, and the graves of her son Edwin (Edward) Butler, her daughter Ester Butler Primas and many of Mahala's grandchildren. So far, the researcher has not found any living relatives of the Butler children.

For Rachel and Joseph, they now know that their family have survived the test of time. They can now rest in peace.

FAYRENE LYLES RICHARDSON

Beckley, Charley—buried July 20, 1864, age six months
Dorsey, Dexius—buried July 31, 1864, age twenty-six
Dorsey, Solomon—buried November 26, 1864, age thirty
Johnson, Sam—buried April 6, 1865, age three

In the summer of 1864, Alexandria experienced a serious drought, and river water levels became extremely low, causing water shortage throughout the city. With the increase of the population of contrabands, the unhealthy conditions and the infestation of mosquitoes were death traps for many in the area. Charley Beckley and Dexius Dorsey died eleven days apart. That same family were hit with two other deaths: Solomon Dorsey died on November 26, 1864, and Sam Johnson died at the end of the Civil War on April 6, 1865. All of them were buried at the Freedmen's Cemetery.

Finding descendants for Charley Beckley, Dexius Dorsey, Soloman Dorsey and Sam Johnson was not difficult. The genealogist worked with Fayrene Lyles Richardson on another project, and the genealogist knew that she was related to the Lyles, Beckley and Dorsey families. Her Lyles and Beckley families were free people of color before the Civil War.

The focus was to find out whether Fayrene's Beckley and Dorsey families were connected to Charley, Dexius and Solomon. Since her paternal side of the family were already documented, the genealogist pursued her paternal great-grandfather, Richard Henry Lyles. In the 1850 census, Richard was listed as a mulatto (mixed race). He was in the household of John Campbell along with his father, William; mother, Hannah; sister, Martha; and another person, James Mitchell.

Because Richard and his family were listed in the 1850 census as free people, they were registered as free people of color in the Negro Registers. Before the Civil War, the law in Virginia stated that all colored people who were free had to register at the county courthouse as free people of color and carry free papers on them to prove their status. An abstract of the Alexandria County, Virginia Free Negro Registers 1797–1861 by Dorothy S. Provine was used to verify whether Richard and his family had registered as free people of color. In Provine's book, Richard and his brother, Turner, were registered on October 22, 1846, as the children of Hannah Smith Lyles, who was a free woman. It was customary that underage children were listed with their mothers. Based on Hannah's entry, it confirmed that she was born free and so were her children. Richard was listed in the 1846

Left: Fayrene Lyles Richardson; *Right*: Reverend Richard H. Lyles. *Courtesy Fayrene Lyles Richardson.*

and 1856 Negro Registers. In 1856, his physical description was also listed as a dark mulatto about twenty-two years old and five feet, seven and a half inches tall. From this information, Richard was researched to identify his connection to the Beckley and Dorsey families.

On October 6, 1856, Richard Henry Lyles married Mary Elizabeth Beckley. Just like Richard, Elizabeth was born free. In the Negro Registers' entry for August 7, 1856, Elizabeth Beckley was described as a bright mulatto (mixed race), about twenty years old and five feet, three inches tall, with no visible marks. This research revealed that the Lyles and Beckley families continued to name their children after the prior generations. All the free Beckley and Lyles families prior to 1865 were kin. Using the marriages, deaths, censuses, Free Negro Registers, United States Freedmen's Bureau records, church records, United States Southern Claims Commission's records and family interviews proved that Fayrene Lyles Richardson is the descendant of Charley Beckley, Dexius Dorsey, Solomon Dorsey and Sam Johnson.

During the Civil War, Richard worked closely with the Freedmen's Bureau as a minister and teacher. He provided education to the free and formerly enslaved people. He also was a caulker on boats and ships that came into

Mary Elizabeth Beckley Lyles and granddaughter Mary Etta. *Courtesy Fayrene Lyles Richardson.*

Alexandria. His wife, Mary Elizabeth Beckley Lyles, had several siblings, one of whom was Rosier (Rozier) Beckley. Rosier and his second wife, Ann Elizabeth Smith, buried Charley Beckley at the Freedmen's Cemetery. Rosier was born in 1835. His father, John Beckley, died prior to 1854. Rosier petitioned the Alexandria court for guardianship of his underage siblings in 1854. He held several positions in his lifetime as United States Post Office Department employee, U.S. assistant assessor of the Fourth Division of the Third District of Virginia, messenger for the federal government and delegate to the Convention of the Colored People of Virginia in 1865. He later moved from 118 Henry Street in Alexandria to 450 Pennsylvania Avenue, NW, in Washington, D.C.

Richard and Elizabeth had a daughter named Hannah. They named her after Richard's mother. On June 4, 1878, Hannah Lyles married Clem M. Dorsey Jr. The Dorsey family came to Alexandria during the Civil War from Charles County, Maryland. Dexius and Soloman, who are buried at the Freedmen's Cemetery, were siblings of Clem Dorsey Jr. The Dorsey family intermarried with the Johnson family. Clem Dorsey Sr. had a sibling named Samuel Dorsey. Samuel Dorsey's daughter married Thomas Johnson, and they buried their three-year-old son, Sam Johnson, at the Freedmen's Cemetery.

The Beckley, Dorsey and Lyles families contributed a lot to the history of Alexandria. Richard H. Lyles became a pastor at Roberts Memorial United Methodist Church (Roberts Chapel), which still has a congregation today. Richard owned property prior to and after the Civil War. In 1900, Richard was living at his property at 616 South Columbus Street. He was a skilled caulker on boats and ships. Richard and Elizabeth's son, Rosier Lyles, was named after Elizabeth's brother, Rosier Beckley. Rosier Lyles became a well-known teacher at the Snowden School for Boys, and he was one of the first teachers to be hired at Parker-Gray School in 1920. He was their math teacher. Richard's daughter, Hannah, had two daughters with Clem Dorsey Jr.: Laura Missouri Dorsey and Mary Dorsey.

Left: Laura M. Dorsey (1879–1968); *Right*: Tonya J. Richardson and brother Eduardo E. Richardson. *Courtesy Fayrene Lyles Richardson.*

Laura followed in the footsteps of her grandfather Richard, who taught school during the Civil War, and her uncle, Rosier. Laura taught at Hallowell School for Girls prior to 1920, and she was one of the first teachers at Parker-Gray School in 1920. Laura retired in the 1940s with more than forty-five years of teaching. John Henry William Lyles was Richard and Elizabeth's oldest child. John had a son with his second wife when he was living in Connecticut. Albert William Lyles was the youngest child of John. On September 8, 1937, Albert married Lillian H. Williams. At the time of their marriage, Albert was living at 319 North Alfred Street. Albert's early occupation was a self-employed barber. His final occupation was a supervisor at the National Cemetery. Albert and his wife had one child: Fayrene. Fayrene was born in 1943. She married Clarence E. Richardson in 1962. They have two children, Tonya J. Richardson and Eduardo E. Richardson. Fayrene also has two grandchildren and three great-grandchildren. She retired from the federal government. Her career was in government acquisition as a contract specialist/negotiator, as well as a human resource specialist. Fayrene also spent many years as a residential real estate investor, owning a number of properties. For more than two hundred years, Fayrene's paternal families have been Methodist, but her maternal families were Baptist. As a child, she was a member of Woodlawn United Methodist Church, but now she is a member of Fort Washington Baptist Church. Finding descendants of the Freedmen's Cemetery brought unknown families together. Fayrene discovered her unknown Beckley cousin, Sherrin Hamilton Bell. They are now catching up on their two-hundred-year history.

For the Beckley, Dorsey and Johnson families who are buried at the Freedmen's Cemetery, they have been found, and what positive impacts they made on the history of Alexandria, Virginia!

BEATRICE CROSS TAYLOR

Baltimore, infant—buried July 5, 1868, stillborn
Baltimore, Maria (twin)—buried December 2, 1864, age one day
Baltimore, Martha (twin)—buried December 2, 1864, age one day
Baltimore, Moses—buried December 27, 1865, age three
Baltimore, Thomas—buried June 14, 1865, age sixty

In late November 1864, the weather was extremely cold, with one inch of ice in the gutters and on the dirt roads. A steady stream of snow flurries came down, setting the stage for December's coldest weather. Twins Maria and Martha Baltimore were born on December 1. The twins only lived for one day. With the ground frozen with ice, they were probably buried at a later date. Between 1864 and 1868, the Baltimores lost five family members, including the twins.

Mrs. Charlene Taylor Napper connected the genealogist to her sister-in-law, who is related to the Baltimore family. Beatrice Cross Taylor's maternal great-grandfather was Frank Baltimore, who was born in 1858 in Warrenton, a town in Fauquier, Virginia. In 1870, Frank was living in First Revenue District of Fauquier, Virginia, in the household of John Downing. He was reported as four years old, but he was actually a little older. Initially, it did not seem that Frank was connected to the individuals who were buried at the Freedmen's Cemetery, but he was. The Cemetery burials started in 1864 and ended in 1868. People who were connected to individuals at the Cemetery had to have had family members in Alexandria during those burial years.

From left to right: Karen Taylor Chandler, Lucy Roy, Beatrice Cross Taylor, John Taylor and Rhonda Taylor. *Courtesy Beatrice Cross Taylor.*

Betsey Baltimore, Thomas Baltimore and Samuel Baltimore migrated from Warrenton in Fauquier, Virginia, during the Civil War. Using marriage certificates, death certificates, Freedmen's Bureau records, United States Census records, oral histories, newspapers, military records, family naming patterns and migration paths of the Baltimore family, the genealogist was able to connect Frank Baltimore to his Aunt Betsey, Great-Uncle Thomas and Uncle Samuel (Sam), who connected to the Freedmen's Cemetery. The Baltimores who were buried at the Freedmen's Cemetery were Betsey's son, Moses, and possibly the stillborn Baltimore child, Thomas Baltimore and Samuel's twins, Maria and Martha Baltimore.

Frank and his siblings arrived after 1870. In the 1880 census, Frank and his siblings, John and Carter, were living in Alexandria in the household of their aunt, Julia, and her son, Henry (William Henry) Whiting. It appeared that Frank's parents had passed away in Warrenton, Virginia, and he and his siblings were sent to Alexandria to live with relatives.

The only known Baltimores who exist in Alexandria today are Frank Baltimore's descendants. The genealogist researched Frank and his living descendants. On October 26, 1882, Frank Baltimore married Lucy Jane Spriggs in Alexandria. Lucy's family were free people of color in Alexandria prior to the Civil War. Lucy Jane Spriggs Baltimore also had family buried at the Freedmen's Cemetery, which will be discussed in the narrative of Sherrin Hamilton Bell. Frank and Lucy's children were Lola, Clinton, Leon, Bessie, Mary and Preston. Frank's wife, Lucy, died after 1896. After 1900, Frank's children lived with his deceased wife's family, the Spriggs, at 600 South Washington Street in Alexandria. Frank was a businessman who owned his own store in Alexandria. An article dated May 22, 1926, in the *Alexandria*

Lucy Carter Cross and daughter Beatrice Cross (1940s). *Courtesy Beatrice Cross Taylor.*

Lucy Carter Cross Roy (1916–2006). *Courtesy Beatrice Cross Taylor.*

Gazette reported a burglary there. The thief took five dollars in cash, cigarettes and a flashlight—further confirmation that Frank had a store. Frank never remarried after his wife's death. On August 13, 1933, Frank died. He was living at 513 Gibbon Street.

Two of Frank's children stayed in Alexandria. His son, Leon, and his daughter, Bessie, left descendants there. Leon Baltimore Sr. became a teacher. His son, Leon Jr., was a well-known electrician and owner of a television repair shop. Leon Jr.'s daughter, Ann Baltimore Flye, lives in Alexandria. On February 17, 1914, Frank's daughter, Bessie Evans Baltimore, married Irving (Irvin) Chesterfield Carter in Washington, D.C. They had two daughters, Verma Evelyn and Lucy Beatrice Carter. Bessie and Irving died young. On December 26, 1918, Bessie Evans Baltimore Carter died at the age of twenty-nine. On March 1, 1920, Irving Chesterfield Carter died at the age of thirty-one (death certificate stated that his age as twenty-eight, which was incorrect). Prior to their death, they were living at 606 South Washington Street. Verma and Lucy were raised by their Carter family. On April 9, 1936, Verma Carter married Sylvester Roy. Verma and Sylvester had four children: Sylvester Jr., Raymond, Donald and Lucy. On December 24, 1934, Lucy Beatrice Carter married Haywood S. Cross. They had one daughter, Beatrice

Virginia Cross. On March 17, 1942, Haywood and Lucy were divorced. Lucy Beatrice Carter Cross remarried in the 1940s to Harold Roy. Harold was Verma's brother-in-law. Lucy and Harold had one son, Harold Roy Jr.

Roy, Daniel—buried July 23, 1866, age fourteen
Roy, Sarah—buried August 12, 1864, age three

Two of the Roy's children died during the hot summer months of 1864 and 1866. Both of these children were related to Verma and Lucy's husbands. Harold and Sylvester Roy's father was Norman Roy. Norman's father was James P. Roy, and Norman's grandparents were Daniel and Sarah Ann Roy. Daniel and his wife buried their fourteen-year-old child, Daniel, at the Freedmen's Cemetery, and their daughter, Evelina, buried her three-year-old child, Sarah.

Verma and Lucy Carter have many relatives who are buried at the Freedmen's Cemetery, including their Franklin, Spriggs and Robinson families. These families will be in the narrative of Verma and Lucy's other relatives.

Lucy continued her membership in the family church until she died in 2006. For more than a century, Roberts Memorial United Methodist Church has been the church of Lucy's Baltimore, Spriggs, Franklin, Carter and Robinson family members. Lucy's daughter, Beatrice Cross Taylor, continues that family legacy today with her daughter, Karen. Beatrice's daughter, Rhonda, is a member of Third Baptist Church in Alexandria. In 1996, Mrs. Taylor retired from the federal government. She spends her time among the church, the community and her family.

For the Baltimore and Roy families who are buried at the Freedmen's Cemetery, you are not forgotten.

From left to right: Donald Roy, Verma Carter Roy, Raymond Roy, Sylvester Roy Jr. and Lucy Roy. *Courtesy Beatrice Cross Taylor.*

SHERRIN HAMILTON BELL

Franklin, Rachael—buried April 16, 1866, age eighty
Franklin, William—buried April 22, 1864, age four months

In the month of April 1866, the weather was rainy and cool, and communities were lighting bonfires and wearing overcoats to keep themselves warm. During a cool and rainy day on April 16, 1866, death claimed Rachel Franklin. The weather was almost identical in 1864, when William Franklin died.

In 2013, the genealogist received an e-mail from Ms. Sherrin Hamilton Bell from Philadelphia, Pennsylvania. She told the genealogist that she was trying to locate the grave of her second great-grandfather George Henry Franklin. Unbeknownst to Sherrin, three descendant families in Alexandria Freedmen's Cemetery are related to George H. Franklin. These descendants were Mrs. Fayrene Lyles Richardson, Mrs. Beatrice Virginia Cross Taylor and Mrs. Carolyn Phillips McCrae. Sherrin was unaware that she was related to these ladies in Alexandria, Virginia. Two of these relatives are members of Roberts Memorial United Methodist Church. More than two hundred years ago, George H. Franklin, his siblings and parents were also members of the same church.

George's family were free people of color in Alexandria before the Civil War. He was born in 1835, and his parents were Robert Franklin Sr. and Nancy Goddard Franklin Hodge; he came from a large family. The Franklin family were located in Alexandria County, Virginia, and were listed in the Free Negro Registers of 1797–1861. The abstract registration in 1856 for George H. Franklin stated that "he was a very dark mulatto, about 21 years old, 5 feet 9 inches tall, with a dark mark on his forehead over his left eye. He was born free, as appears by evidence of Henry Hallowell."

George's father, Robert, had amassed a great deal of property prior to 1865. It appears that he was a free man, but he was not listed in the Alexandria County, Virginia Free Negro Registers. The genealogist connected George H. Franklin to Rachel and William of the Freedmen's Cemetery through George's father, Robert Franklin Sr. Robert was born in the 1790s in Alexandria, Virginia, when the city became part of Washington, D.C., before it returned to Virginia in 1846. During that period, Robert Franklin Sr. met a former slave, Nancy Goddard, and they married and had a number of children. In order to find any record on him, the genealogist had to include the District of Columbia prior to

Left: George H. Franklin's son, Harry Franklin (1870–1901); *Right*: Harry Franklin's daughter, Helen F. Franklin (1898–1979). *Courtesy Sherrin Hamilton Bell.*

1846. The genealogist researched marriage records, Free Negro Registers, death certificates, cemetery headstones, census records, family interviews, migration patterns, tax records, newspapers and a 574-page Chancery Court (Equity Court) that involved the late Robert Franklin Sr. and his late wife, Nancy Goddard Franklin Hodge, and their children, as well as the Seaton family. The result of the research revealed that Robert Franklin Sr. was the brother of Rachel Franklin and the grandfather of William Franklin, both of whom were buried at the Freedmen's Cemetery.

On the 1865 Personal Property Tax record in Alexandria, George's father Robert Franklin's estate taxes were on three houses and several parcels of land at Washington and Gibbon Streets assessed at $1,500. George also paid taxes on his house at Duke and Columbus Streets assessed at $200. In August 1865, George was a delegate to the Convention of the Colored People of Virginia. On June 21, 1869, George H. Franklin married Sarah Ellen Beckley in Alexandria. Sarah was first cousin to Rosier Beckley, who buried his child at the Freedmen's Cemetery. This connection confirmed that Sherrin Hamilton Bell and Fayrene Lyles Richardson are related.

Sprague, Maria—buried October 27, 1866, age twenty-five
Spriggs, Ben—buried January 31, 1865, age unknown
Spriggs, George—buried December 1, 1864, age twenty-three
Spriggs, infant—buried June 26, 1866, age three weeks
Spriggs, infant—buried February 14, 1868, age five weeks

George H. Franklin had a sister, Mary Franklin, who married Daniel Spriggs before the Civil War. Daniel was born in 1835, and his wife, Mary, was born in 1839. Daniel had a brother, Fielding Spriggs, who was born around 1820; another brother, George, who was born around 1841; and a sister, Julia. Maria, Ben and a three-week-old infant were buried by Fielding Spriggs at the Freedmen's Cemetery. Daniel's sister, Julia, buried her five-week-old infant at the Cemetery. Daniel's brother, George, was in the military and died in the L'Ouverture Hospital in Alexandria, and he was originally buried at the Freedmen's Cemetery until his remains were moved to the National Veterans Cemetery in Alexandria. This research was confirmed through censuses, marriage records, death certificates, cemetery records, city directories, tax records and military records.

2014 Freedmen's Cemetery Descendants' Banquet. *From left to right*: Derrick Walton, Andrea Walton Reid, Corrin Franklin Reid and Sherrin Hamilton Bell. *Courtesy Tisara Photography.*

In 1911, Mary Franklin Spriggs; her daughters, Bessie and Nannie; and her grandchildren, Leon Baltimore and his siblings, were all living at 600 South Washington Street in Alexandria, Virginia. Descendants Sherrin Hamilton Bell, Fayrene Lyles Richardson, Beatrice Virginia Cross Taylor and Carolyn Phillips McCrae are related to one another through the Franklins, Spriggs, Baltimore and Beckley families. They all are related to Mary Franklin Spriggs.

Sherrin's second great-grandfather George Henry Franklin left Alexandria before 1900 and moved to Washington, D.C. He died in 1922, but he was buried in Alexandria near his wife and children. George's son, Harry Franklin, died in 1901; he was Sherrin's great-grandfather. Harry is buried in Alexandria. Sherrin's grandmother Helen Franklin Hamilton was born in St. Paul, Minnesota, and died in 1979. Sherrin's mother, Helen Louise Hamilton Bell, was born in Washington, D.C., and died in 2012.

Sherrin was born in Philadelphia, and that is where she still resides. She is a retired personnel analyst for the Commonwealth of Pennsylvania. A graduate of Cheyney University of Pennsylvania, a historically black college, Sherrin is the oldest granddaughter of Helen Franklin Hamilton. She now devotes her time to her fine arts talents.

The Franklins and Spriggs families now know how they are connected to their ancestors buried at the Freedmen's Cemetery.

CAROLYN PHILLIPS MCCRAE

Brent, Leonard—buried March 1, 1866, age nine
Gaines, William—buried November 5, 1864, age twenty-four

The arrival of early spring in 1866 gave the communities an early start on their gardens and lots by preparing the grounds for early planting. For Leonard Brent, his short life ended at the L'Ouverture Hospital in Alexandria during the planting season on the first day of March. William Gaines also died on a warm day in November at the L'Ouverture Hospital, and he was buried on November 5, 1864.

An unsuspected descendant for Leonard Brent and William Gaines located the genealogist to research her family history. Mrs. Carolyn Phillips McCrae was curious to know about the people recorded in her family Bible. Prior to her Aunt Lillian Hodge Spencer's death, she had given Carolyn the 1860 family

Bible without any explanation of how the family were connected to the marriage certificate and death information written in the Bible. Carolyn's aunt never talked about the family history. What Carolyn knew was that her mother and aunt's maiden name was Hodge; the 1869 marriage certificate in the Bible was for Robert Louis Gaines and Hannah Hodge. The witnesses of the marriage were James M. Buckner and Lucy Hodge. Carolyn knew that the Hodges were related, but she did not know how they were related to her. Carolyn Phillips McCrae then contacted the genealogist to find her family connection. Through the research process, it was discovered that Carolyn's family history goes back more than two hundred years in Alexandria and that several of her relatives were buried at the Alexandria Freedmen's Cemetery. Beyond Carolyn's Baltimore, Franklin and Spriggs families, she is also connected to the Brent and the Hodge families.

Details on Carolyn's family were contained in many records: marriage certificates, birth records, census records, family interviews, Bible records, church records, free registry, city directories, tax records, newspaper articles, school records, and a 574-page Chancery Case (Equity Court) case that involved the late Robert Franklin Sr. and his late wife, Nancy Goddard Franklin Hodge. In this process, it was found that Carolyn was connected to the Middleton, Hodge, Brent, Franklin, Spriggs and the Baltimore families.

Lillian Eloise Simmons Spencer (1922–2001). *Courtesy Carolyn Phillips McCrae.*

Courtney Mae Hodge Reynolds (1928–2002). *Courtesy Carolyn Phillips McCrae.*

Her early ancestors were David Middleton and Hannah Harris Middleton. They were married on June 24, 1830. On the 1840 census, David was living in Washington, D.C., in the section that was part of Alexandria, Virginia. In his household were five free people of color. In 1846, Alexandria returned to Virginia. David and his wife, Hannah, were registered in the Alexandria County, Virginia Free Negro Registers. David was registered on August 7, 1847. A free man, he was fifty-six years of age; five feet, seven inches tall; and of a black complexion, with a scar in the palm of his left hand. His wife, Hannah Middleton, was registered on March 19, 1847. She was forty-five years of age; five feet, four inches tall; and had a dark complexion and a scar on her left thumb. She was free. In February 1850, David was in an accident in which he was crushed to death. Hannah was left to raise their children, David Jr., Hannah, Jane, Mary and Isabella. They appeared on the 1850, 1860 and 1870 censuses. Two of Hannah's children married men who were connected to the Alexandria Freedmen's Cemetery.

Hannah's daughter, Mary Middleton, married Charles Hodge in 1871. Mary and Charles were Carolyn's great-grandparents. Charles's parents were Moses and Harriet; they also had a daughter, Hannah Hodge. One of the witnesses to Hannah Hodge Gaines's wedding was Lucy Hodge. Lucy's parents were Thomas Hodge and Nancy Goddard Franklin Hodge. Thomas Hodge was Moses's brother, and Moses was Hannah Hodge Gaines's father. This relationship connected Carolyn Phillips McCrae to the Hodge and Gaines families mentioned in the family Bible.

Prior to Robert Gaines's marriage to Hannah Hodge in 1869, he and his brother, William Gaines, migrated during the Civil War from Louisa, Virginia, to Alexandria, Virginia, where they both became contrabands. During that time, Robert's brother, William Gaines, died at L'Ouverture Hospital in Alexandria, and he was buried at the Freedmen's Cemetery.

Carolyn Phillips McCrae's great-grandmother Mary Middleton Hodge's sister, Lillie Middleton, had a daughter named Carrie Middleton. Carrie Middleton married Thomas Bent in 1905. William Thomas Brent and Hannah Brown Brent were Thomas's parents. William and his wife, Hannah, were brought to Alexandria by their slave owner, Dr. George Washington Brent, prior to 1860. During the Civil War, William and his wife were declared contrabands of war. On March 1, 1866, their son, Leonard, died and was buried at the Freedmen's Cemetery. After Leonard's death, William Thomas Brent and his wife, Hannah Brent, returned to Culpeper, Virginia. While in Culpeper, the Brents had another son, Thomas Brent

Bessie Hodge Simmons (1879–1950). *Courtesy Carolyn Phillips McCrae.*

Jr. Prior to 1900, Thomas Jr. migrated to Alexandria, Virginia, where he met Carrie Middleton.

Mrs. McCrae's grandmother Bessie Hodge Simmons had three children: Charles, Florence and Lillie. Carolyn's aunt, Lillie, was the one who gave her the family Bible. Florence Hodge McKenney (McKenny) had four children: Courtney, Earl, Carolyn and Clarence. Only Carolyn and her brother Clarence are living.

Carolyn Phillips McCrae and her husband, Daniel Morgan McCrae. *Courtesy Tisara Photography.*

Carolyn Phillips McCrae was born in 1938. Her parents were Florence Hodge and Mathew Phillips. He died in 1942. Florence was a domestic worker who worked hard to support her family. She later married Mr. Clarence McKenney. Florence died in 1959. Carolyn was raised by Mrs. Jenny Bell Canty (Cantey), who was her babysitter and foster mother. Carolyn fondly called Mrs. Canty "Mama." Mama raised not only Carolyn but also Clarence Milton, another child she kept. Carolyn and Clarence grew up as siblings. Unknown to Carolyn, Clarence really was her cousin. His family name got misspelled from "Middleton" to "Milton." After Clarence left home, Carolyn and Mama moved to 719 North Alfred Street. Clarence served in World War II. While he was in the military, he sent savings bonds to Mama. She never used the savings bonds. Mama died in 1961 at the age of 102. After the death of Mama, Clarence shared the savings bonds with Carolyn, and after she graduated from Parker-Gray High School in 1957, she used the bonds to attend business school. While attending business school, she babysat and did domestic work. She was the only member in her family who graduated from high school and furthered her education. She retired from the federal government after forty-two years of service.

Carolyn received many awards and commendations for her excellent work performance. Mama would have been proud of her.

Mrs. McCrae has always known that she was related to the Brent family, but she did not know how. When Mrs. Carolyn Phillips McCrae inherited the family Bible, she was given her family history.

For more than 250 years, Carolyn's Middleton, Hodge and Franklin families have lived in Alexandria and attended the same church. They were members of a white Methodist church called Trinity until the black members left and started their own Methodist church in 1832. The church has gone through several names: from Davis Chapel to Roberts Chapel and now Roberts Memorial United Methodist Church. From Trinity to Roberts, Carolyn's ancestors witnessed the church's history through the years.

Mrs. McCrae lives in Maryland with her husband, Daniel (Dan) Morgan McCrae. She has now reconnected her ancestors from the family Bible to the Freedmen's Cemetery.

GWEN BROWN HENDERSON

Brooks, William—buried May 6, 1865, age fifty-five
Brown, infant—buried February 5, 1866, age one week
Payne, Celia—buried May 16, 1867, age fourteen

At the end of April, heavy rains poured down from the sky for several days. On May 6, 1865, the weather changed to a beautiful, warm spring day. Plants came alive, trees were full of leaves and the flowers bloomed—also, the life of William Brooks ended on that spring day. Just like William, Celia Payne died on a nice spring day on May 16, 1867. Celia and William's lives were in contrast to the one-week-old Brown infant who died in the winter of 1866.

A casual conversation with a colleague, Gwen Brown Henderson, on her family history sparked interest in this genealogist to research Gwen's family. The research revealed that her family connected to several people buried at the Freedmen's Cemetery through direct and indirect lines. This research started with her mother, Frances Katherine Brown, by using all the state, federal and county records that were available, including oral history interviews.

Frances K. Brown was born in 1911 to Alfred (Albert) Brown Jr. and Mary Ellen Payne in Alexandria, Virginia. Albert Brown's given name was

Frances Katherine Brown (*standing*).
Courtesy Gwen Brown Henderson.

incorrectly listed as "Alfred" on Frances's death certificate. In Albert's own words on his marriage license, his full name was Albert Brown Jr., and his parents were Albert Brown Sr. and Amanda Clannagan. Albert Sr. married a widow, Amanda Clannagan Blandon, on January 4, 1866; their first child was born the following month. The infant lived for one week and was buried at the Freedmen's Cemetery on February 5, 1866.

On May 15, 1884, Amanda married her third husband, George Brooks. She stated her previous marriage status as single, and she also appeared to be much younger than in her first two marriages. George's parents were William and Elizabeth. George's father, William, lived long enough to witness Alexandria declare all slaves free. He died thirteen months later, on May 6, 1865. He is buried at the Freedmen's Cemetery.

Amanda made one final trip to the preacher, marrying her fourth husband, George Wanzer, on September 1, 1890. Just like in Amanda's first three marriages, she continued to maintain that her age was in the twenties. George and his parents were in Fauquier, Virginia, during the Civil War, but his father had relatives who were in Alexandria during the Civil War. Those relatives connected to the Freedmen's Cemetery, and they will be discussed in Frances Terrell and Gerald Wanzer's narrative.

Gwen's great-grandmother Delilah Payne had a sister named Fannie. Fannie made the arrangements for Celia to be buried at the Freedmen's Cemetery. Delilah, Celia, Sallie and Fannie were Susan Payne Washington's children. Susan migrated to Alexandria from West Virginia during the Civil War.

Gibson, Albert—buried September 1, 1866, age three
Gibson, infant—buried September 24, 1867, age eleven months

On August 1, 1892, widower Aaron Gibson, a blacksmith, married the widow Mary Clanaken (Clannagan). Mary was Amanda Clannagan Brown's mother. Aaron Gibson was listed on the burial records as the father of the three-year-old Albert Gibson at the Freedmen's Cemetery. Aaron's first wife, Elizabeth, was listed as the mother of the eleven-month-old infant at the Freedmen's Cemetery.

The genealogist researched Gwen's maternal side, revealing her connections to the Freedmen's Cemetery. Frances K. Brown and her children had more opportunities than their ancestors. They took advantage of those opportunities and devoted their careers to public service.

Frances had three children: Helen L. Brown Jones, Eugene T. Brown and Gwendolyn (Gwen) Brown Henderson. Frances's son, Eugene, who is deceased, was a local singer with the Embraceables in the Northern Virginia area. Frances's

Gwen Brown Henderson. *Courtesy Tisara Photography.*

daughter Helen, who is deceased, worked for the federal government at the Government Printing Office. Helen's daughter Jocelyn Jones Travers is retired from the Department of Navy. Helen's two other daughters, Pamela Jones and Helen Jones, are deceased. Frances K. Brown retired from the House of Representatives. She was living at 900 Wolfe Street when she died on September 23, 1979.

Gwen is the only surviving child of Frances. Gwen was the first generation in her family to finish high school. She graduated from T.C. Williams High School in 1968 and continued her education at Northern Virginia Community College. After she left school, Gwen started working for the federal government at the U.S. Department of State. She retired from the department with forty-one years of service. Gwen has one daughter, Nichole Beatty, who has been working at Ortho Virginia Company for eighteen years as an X-ray technician.

Gwen Brown Henderson was not aware that she had ancestors buried at the Freedmen's Cemetery. She has direct and indirect relatives among the Brooks, Brown, Payne, Wanzer and Gibson families. Gwen has a newfound appreciation for the Freedmen's Cemetery, as she now knows that her family were in Alexandria during the Civil War and witnessed the end of slavery.

Chapter 2

DON'T FORGET ABOUT ME

I speak for all of us who are buried in this place. It has been a long time since the Civil War ended. We have been in this grave for more than 150 years. Our graves have been violated throughout the years. Before we die, we ask that our families do not forget about us.

Within the first several years after the Civil War, our resting place has been used as a dumping site. We heard the seagulls above our graves pecking through the waste that people had dumped. Then we started smelling the gasoline and the concrete. We heard the construction and the sound of bricks and concrete being laid. Then we realized that a gas station was now on top of our graves. No one remembered us. We were all forgotten. We could not hear the birds or feel the tree roots anymore. Oh Lord, did they forget about us?

Before the gas station was built, no family members visited us and no flowers were placed on our graves. Did they forget about us—Oh Lord, did they forget about us?

Do you remember when we came to Alexandria for refuge, seeking a place of safety from the Confederates until the war was over? Unknown to many of us, this was the end of our lives. Our bodies, minds and souls have been used and abused from the day we were born. By the time freedom arrived, our bodies were already worn out. Our children were born weak from lack of nutrition; they were destined to be dead on arrival. Curable diseases were unable to be cured because of malnourished bodies. The old and the very young were dying by the hundreds every year. But life without freedom is death without a grave. Do not forget about us.

We remembered the war when freed people were afraid that they would be captured by the Confederates and sold into slavery again. We remembered every day of our living lives, of the miserable state of slavery, the pain of all the injustices and the sorrows of losing our families. When the war started, we were going to take our chances—death or freedom.

We left old master's plantation running as fast as we could to the Union side. Our babies were sick and our bodies were tired, but we just had to get our freedom here on earth or over yonder, where we will see Jesus. We followed the Union soldiers until we got to Alexandria, and there we stayed until death claimed each and every one of us. Many of us didn't live long enough to hear that we were free, but the ones who did rejoiced that there was no more slavery. Sickness fell on our bodies and our children's bodies; many of us lived long enough to bury our children. But when it was our time to go, we felt the warmth of the sun, the coolness of the weather and the somber feeling of our family around us. One after another, we whispered to our families before we left this world: "Don't forget about us. Don't forget what we have been through. You are free, we are dying for your freedom, so that you can have a better life. Do not forget about us."

We have been worked like mules from sunup to sundown, and we have witnessed the animals eating the finest foods when we were near starvation. Yes, we suffered in this world, but now we are free to make a better world. Remember our journey, remember our struggle and remember not to forget about us. This Cemetery is a testimony to all who wanted to be free. We wanted the pleasures of life like all human beings. We wanted our children to be educated, to have their own home, to have paying jobs and to have control over their lives. Yes, we wanted all those things if it meant dying to get them—it was worth the sacrifice. As we listen to the traffic passing by the gas station, we wonder whether anyone remembers the war. Do they remember that we are buried here? Will they remember us?

It has been a long time since we have been among the living; do not forget about us. We are waiting to hear your laughter, to smell your fresh scented bodies, to see what you look like, to hear about your successes. We want to know that our sacrifices for your freedom gave you everything that we wanted. We want you to remember our struggles and our fight for freedom. Do not take your freedom for granted. Remember that we died for you to be free. Do not forget about us.

FRANCES NORTON BURTON

Norton, William Henry—buried August 8, 1866, age eight months

During the unusually pleasant temperatures on August 8, 1866, baby William Henry Norton died. His body was brought to the Freedmen's Cemetery by his mother, Sarah Norton.

In 2011, Frances (Fran) Norton Burton prepared for a family reunion. During her preparation for the reunion, her cousin Beatrice Cross Taylor suggested to her that she should get a genealogist to research their family.

Fran informed this author-genealogist that her paternal grandparents were Henry A. Norton and Dora Nash Norton. Fran discovered through the genealogist that a child, William Henry Norton, was buried at the Alexandria Freedmen's Cemetery.

Using primary and secondary source documents, marriage certificates, death certificates, church records, land records, cemetery records, Freedmen's Bureau records and census records, this author concluded that Fran had two relatives buried at the Freedmen's Cemetery—one on her mother's side and the other on her father's side.

Many of the burial records did not include the names of the deceased family member, but the Norton and Nash records named the mother of the person who was buried. Dora Nash Norton was from Gainesville, Virginia. The Nash burial will be discussed in Ronald Burke's narrative. For the Norton family, the discovery of baby, William Henry Norton, revealed family history that was unknown.

While the genealogist was researching the young child at the Cemetery, Sarah Norton's name was discovered on the 1870 census with her husband, Henry (Henley). In the household were three children: Lavinia, age seven;

Dora Nash Norton (*second row, fourth from left*) with the Norton family. *Courtesy Frances Norton Burton.*

Charles, age two; and Susan, age two months. Given the year of his birth, it appeared that William Henry Norton was the second child of Henry and Sarah. In looking at the 1880 census, Henry and Sarah had three more children in the family: Mary, Henry and George.

Henry and Sarah's children were researched to see whether they connected to Fran Norton Burton. Their son Henry A. Norton became a focal point in the research because Fran had previously informed the genealogist that she knew her grandparents were Henry A. Norton and Dora Nash Norton. A marriage license dated July 20, 1899, for Henry A. Norton and Dora Nash proved that

Frances Norton Burton and son Reuben Anthony Burton. *Courtesy Frances Norton Burton.*

Henry's parents were Henry (Henley) and Sarah Norton. Henry A. Norton was the brother of the baby, William Henry Norton, and Henry was Fran's grandfather. Henry and his wife had many children, including their first two sons, both named William Henry, who died in infancy. Fran's father, Arthur O. Norton Sr., is Henry A. Norton's son.

Henry A. and Dora Norton, lived at 228 North Payne Street after they married. Henry worked for the brickyard as a brick maker. In 1910, Henry and Dora and their children lived at 607½ South Columbus Street. His occupation was a laborer. By 1930, they had had eight children and were still living at South Columbus Street. Henry landed a job at the navy yard.

For every generation since the Civil War, a Norton male child was named Henry. Today, Arthur O. Norton Jr. has a young grandson whose name is Max Henry.

The Norton family have accomplished a lot since the death of baby William Henry Norton. William Henry's brother Henry A. was widely known throughout the metropolitan area as the first director of the Twentieth Century Choir and a trustee in the early years of Shiloh Baptist Church in Alexandria. Henry's wife, Dora, was a faithful member of the church, and she was also active in raising her own children. Henry A. Norton died in 1937. Dora lived until 1972 and died at the age of ninety-five.

Norton family at the 2014 Alexandria Freedmen's Cemetery Banquet. *Courtesy Tisara Photography.*

Henry and Dora's grandchildren and great-grandchildren had many opportunities that were not available to their generation—or even to the previous generation. Seven grandchildren and their families' achievements are highlighted.

Arthur O. Norton Jr. obtained his associate degree in applied science, business management, from Northern Virginia Community College. He was drafted into the United States Army and honorably discharged in 1971. He retired from Washington Metropolitan Transit in Washington, D.C., in 1996 with thirty years of service. He is currently a part-time tour guide for the Kennedy Space Center. He holds membership in the Knights of Columbus Council No. 6125, Rockledge, Florida, Third Degree. His children are Romana Norton, who has a PhD in psychology; Arthur O. Norton III, who has a Bachelor of Science degree; Celie Crandall, who is a senior manager at Hilton Worldwide; and Francina L. Schmitt, who has a Bachelor of Arts in Christian ministries. His grandchildren are also on their way to higher education.

Frances Norton Burton worked for the California State Senate as a health and human services policy consultant for two presidents pro tempore. Prior to her retirement, she served two governors and was associate secretary of programs and legislation for the Health and Human Services Agency,

Frances Norton Burton interviewed by Derrick Ward, reporter NBC4. *Courtesy Tisara Photography.*

deputy director for the Department of Alcohol and Drug Programs and deputy director for the Department of Health Services. Currently, she has been appointed by the California State Senate as a public member of the Dental Board of California, where she is serving as vice-president. Fran served two terms as president and was the first African American woman and first public member to serve in that capacity in the board's history. She holds a master's degree in social work. Fran's son, Reuben Anthony Burton, holds a Bachelor of Science degree in occupational safety and health fire science and is a fire apparatus engineer in Nevada County, California.

Jan Norton Hailes graduated from Calvin Coolidge High School in Washington, D.C., and has pursued higher education. Prior to retirement, she held positions with AMTRAK and Levy Sports and Entertainment. Jan's daughter, Robyn Frances Reyes, is a certificated surgical technologist and has a Bachelor of Science degree in nursing. She is a registered nurse at the Washington Hospital Center. Jan has two grandchildren; the youngest has earned her certificate as a dental assistant.

Elbert Norton Jr. graduated from Parker-Gray High School in 1951 and was in the last graduating class of Storer College in Harpers Ferry, West

Virginia, in 1955. He has a Bachelor of Science degree in biology. He is retired from the United States Postal Service. He and his wife, Katherine, met in college and were married for fifty-two years prior to her death. Their children are Angie and Adrian, who is a musician. Elbert has two grandchildren.

Henry B. Norton graduated from Parker-Gray High School in 1954 and graduated with a Bachelor of Science in biology from Virginia State University, where he was also a second lieutenant in the ROTC. He retired after twenty years as a major in the United States Army after a distinguished career, earning two Bronze Stars, two Meritorious Service Medals and a Combat Infantry Parachutist Badge. He did tours of duty in Vietnam, Germany and Korea and was stationed in various states prior to retirement. Henry has four children and six grandchildren.

Roland Norton is deceased. He is survived by three children. His son has been a chaplain for the U.S. Marine Corps and the United States Navy and has advanced degrees in religious education.

Oliver Norton graduated from Parker-Gray High School in 1960. He and his high school sweetheart, Ruth, have been married for fifty-five years. Oliver is an ordained deacon at Shiloh Baptist Church. He has four children, three of whom were college educated. He has three grandchildren.

Frances (Fran) Norton Burton and her siblings' maternal side is represented by the Carters and the Robinsons. A Robinson child buried at the Freedmen's Cemetery connects Fran and her siblings.

Robinson, Leanna—buried August 16, 1865, age six

The maternal side of Frances (Fran) Norton Burton's families were the Carter and the Robinson families. Her mother was Mamie Francenea Carter Norton, and her grandparents were Douglas Carter and Elizabeth Campbell. Her great-grandparents were called Daddy Bill and Baw. The genealogist researched and found that her great-grandparents were named William A. (Bill) and Hester (Baw). Unbeknownst to the family, Hester's maiden name was Robinson, and she was born in 1855 in Alexandria, Virginia. Through Hester's marriages, the genealogist was able to identify Hester's mother. Hester's first marriage was to J.C. Tancil on May 6, 1875. Only one parent was mentioned: her mother, Leanna Robinson. From that marriage were two daughters: Mary Jane (Jim) Tancil and Ellen Tancil. Hester's second marriage was to William A. Carter on December 6, 1883. She mentioned that her mother was Leanna and her father was George H.

Hester and her mother were born in Alexandria. She and her mother are believed to be the former slaves of Daniel H. Hooe and Mary Dade Hooe of Alexandria—Daniel Hooe married his cousin. Daniel came to Alexandria from Prince William, Virginia. It is not known how Daniel and Mary obtained Leanna, but Hester was probably born in the Hooes' household. Hester and Leanna were not free prior to the Civil War. They stayed with the Hooe family until the death of Mary D. Hooe in 1872. The Hooe family had relatives in Frederick, King George, Loudoun, Prince William and Westmoreland Counties in Virginia. Leanna and Hester had a very interesting history. Hester was the niece to free people of color.

In 1861, the Negro Register listed two women registered as free people of color: Lucy Robinson and Louisa Robinson. The description of Lucy Robinson in the register was that she was a thirty-four-year-old dark mulatto and five feet, five inches tall, with a scar on her right arm near her wrist and another at the base of her nose. She was the former slave of Henry Robinson of Frederick County, Virginia. Louisa Robinson was described as a forty-one-year-old bright mulatto at five feet, four and three-fourths inches tall, with a scar over her right eye and another on the inside of her right forefinger. Further research revealed that these two ladies were sisters and the aunts of Hester Robinson.

Lucy and Louisa Robinson were emancipated by their uncle, Henry Robinson, upon the death of their father, Munday (Monday) Robinson, in Frederick, Virginia. Munday was a free Negro who owned his own family. In his will, he made provisions to free his sons at his death, but he made no provisions for the freedom of his daughters. Munday's brother, Henry, freed all of Munday's children and Munday's wife, Polly.

After Lucy and Louisa obtained their freedom, they migrated from Frederick, Virginia, to Alexandria, Virginia. While in Alexandria, Lucy gave birth to a child named Leanna. It is believed that Leanna was named after Hester's mother. In 1864, the child Leanna became ill with smallpox and was hospitalized at the Claremont Smallpox

Hester (Baw) Robinson Tancil Carter (1855–1922). *Courtesy Frances Norton Burton.*

Hospital, located about three miles from Alexandria. The child Leanna was documented as a three-year-old who entered the hospital on July 24, 1864, with smallpox. She was released on January 8, 1865. By August 16, 1865, seven months after she was released, Leanna had died. She was buried at the Alexandria Freedmen's Cemetery. Her death age was listed as six years old. Since she was not listed with her mother on the free register, she was probably born in 1861, which would have made her three years old when she was in the smallpox hospital.

Four documented facts confirmed that Hester shared kinship with Lucy Robinson. The first document was the 1870 census showing that Mary Hooe had three African Americans living in her household: Lucy Robinson, Leanna Robinson and Hester (Esta) Robinson, all of whom were listed as domestic servants. The second document was Mary Hooe's will, in which she left her faithful servants Lucy, Leanna and Hester $1,000 to share equally among them. The third document proving that Hester connected to Lucy and Louisa was a death announcement in the *Alexandria Gazette* on December 17, 1910, announcing that Lucy Robinson was the niece of Hester Carter and that Lucy's funeral would be at the Carter residence. That single article confirmed the kinship between Hester and Lucy. Lastly, Lucy was buried in Alexandria in the family's plot. Over the years, Hester and her children visited Lucy's grave, but neither of them explained to the younger generation who Lucy Robinson was. With these confirmations, Fran shed tears of joy and sadness knowing that another baby from their family was found and buried at the Freedmen's Cemetery.

Little Leanna's relatives have accomplished a great deal since her death. Fran, Arthur and Jan Norton's accomplishments were included in the Norton's narrative. Two more of Hester's great-grandchildren's achievements are highlighted.

Lawrence Oliver Carter is the great-grandson of Hester Robinson Carter. Lawrence retired from the Library of Congress after thirty-eight years of service as an automated operations coordinator. He attended St. Joseph's Catholic Elementary School, and he is a 1965 graduate of Parker-Gray High School. He attended Howard University and Northern Virginia Community College, where he obtained an applied associate degree in data processing and computer programming. Also, he has a diploma in computer programming and system analysis. Lawrence is the second son of Paul Nevell Carter Sr. and Sarah Ann Nelson Carter. His oldest brother, Paul Nevell Carter Jr, is deceased. His other siblings are Joyce Cecilia Carter Thomas and David Alan Carter. Lawrence is married to Elizabeth Althea

2017 Carter-Robinson family picture. *Courtesy Frances Norton Burton.*

Paul Nevell Carter Sr. and Sarah Newman Carter's family. *Courtesy Lawrence O. Carter.*

Above: 2014 attendees at the Freedmen's Cemetery Dedication Ceremony. *Courtesy Tisara Photography.*

Left: Elizabeth Goods Brooks Evans (*far right*) and siblings Todd, Mary and Moses Jr. *Courtesy Elizabeth Evans.*

Proctor, and they have three children: Lawrence Oliver Carter Jr., Yolanda Monique Carter McDaniel and Chrystal René Carter Crawford. Lawrence and his wife have five grandchildren. He is now a member and usher of St. Mary's Catholic Church in Piscataway, Maryland.

Elizabeth Goods Brooks Evans is the great-granddaughter of Hester Robinson Carter. She retired as a supervisor of consumer services and consumer education specialist in Washington, D.C. After retiring, she was appointed as a Montgomery County Executive to serve as a commissioner on aging, where she worked with the Committee on Communications and Outreach. In 1954, she graduated from St. Joseph's Catholic Elementary School in Alexandria, Virginia, and went on to graduate from St. Mary's Academy for Girls in Alexandria. She attended Hampton Institute (University), majoring in elementary education. Interrupting her schooling for marriage and children, she later returned to school to earn an undergrad degree in 1972 and a master's in counseling from the University of Virginia in 1976. Elizabeth is the daughter of Ellen Carter Goods. Elizabeth's siblings are Mary Goods James, Todd Lewis Goods and Moses W. Goods Jr.—all deceased. Elizabeth has four children: Lisa Brooks, Freddie Brooks Jr., Kelli Brooks Carrington and David Evans. Elizabeth has eight grandchildren. She lives in Silver Spring, Maryland.

Fran Norton Burton, Arthur O. Norton Sr., Jan Norton, Lawrence Carter and Elizabeth Goods Brooks Evans—the great-grandchildren of Hester—never knew any of their Robinson history. Baby William Henry Norton and little Leanna Robinson, both of whom had very short lives, were able to bring their family together even in death.

RONALD EUGENE BURKE

Burke, Edmonia—buried August 6, 1864, age seven
Burke, Sally—buried August 14, 1865, age ten months
Burke, William—buried April 22, 1866, age nineteen
Nash, infant—buried April 11, 1866, age one month

Heavy showers brought cool weather and muddy roads on the burial day of William Burke on April 22, 1866. One Nash child and two other Burke children had preceded William in death, and now they were all together.

In Alexandria and in the Northern Virginia area, there are several African American Burke families. Mr. Harry Burke is a well-known Burke

Ronald Burke Sr. with family Annette, Robin and Ronald Jr. *Courtesy the Burke family.*

family member. He is in his nineties. Due to Mr. Harry Burke's health, his cousin Mr. Ronald E. Burke was contacted about the Burke family history. Ronald knew about his great-grandparents John and Sarah Nash Burke in Alexandria. His story corroborated what was found in the censuses, marriages, death certificates, tax records, newspaper articles, Free Negro Registers and chancery court records. With information from these records, the genealogist/author found interesting history on Harry and Ronald Burke's family and found that the Burke children and the Nash child buried at the Cemetery were their relatives.

The research revealed that a slave owner, William Henry Fitzhugh, left instructions in his will to free his slaves after his death. In Fitzhugh's 1830 will, he stated that all his slaves should be free after 1850. Also, Fitzhugh instructed in his will that his emancipated slaves should be given money for their passage to Liberia, West Africa.

The Fitzhugh family had numerous properties in Stafford, Prince William, Fairfax and Alexandria. A group of former slaves of William Henry Fitzhugh retained the surname Burke. They were listed in Fitzhugh's property inventory in family units. They came from Fitzhugh's Prince William, Stafford and

Fairfax plantations. One plantation in Fairfax was named Ravensworth. Those former slaves who were buried at the Freedmen's Cemetery were the children of the former slaves of William Henry Fitzhugh. William's executor of his estate, Silas Burke, emancipated Fitzhugh's slaves. Two of these former slaves were noted in the Free Negro Registers. In 1850: "William Henry Burke a bright mulatto, about 36-years old, 5 feet 7 inches tall, with a scar across his nose and two scars on his forehead was emancipated in the will of William H. Fitzhugh and identified by Col. Silas Burke." And in 1858: "John Burke is a bright mulatto, about 59-years old, 5 feet 9 inches tall, with his left leg and foot contracted from birth. He was emancipated by the will of William H. Fitzhugh of Fairfax County." The two emancipated slaves, William Henry Burke and John Burke, were siblings. The connection to the Freedmen's Cemetery was through William Henry Burke.

William had several children who continued to work on the Fitzhugh plantation in Fairfax and in Prince William, Virginia, after they were emancipated. William's son, John, worked at the Fitzhugh plantation in Prince William County, Virginia, after 1850. While John was in Prince William County, he met his future wife, Sarah Nash. John's father, William, was working in Alexandria prior to the Civil War for Mrs. Anna M. Fitzhugh at her Alexandria estate. William was a witness for Mrs. Fitzhugh when she made a claim to the federal government for property loss during the Civil War. William's testimony in the claim confirmed that he was the former slave of the Fitzhugh family.

When the Civil War started, the children and grandchildren of William moved to Alexandria, Virginia, to be protected by the Union soldiers. William and his children buried their family members at the Cemetery during the Civil War. The nineteen-year-old William Burke who is buried at the Cemetery was William H. Burke's son. The parents of the ten-month-old child, Sally, were John and Sarah (Sallie) Nash Burke. Also, the child was William H. Burke's granddaughter. The other Burke child, Edmonia, is believed to be William's child, grandchild or niece.

The Nash infant buried at the Cemetery was a relative of Sarah Nash Burke's. Several of Sarah's relatives came from Prince William County, Virginia, to live with John and Sarah after the deaths of their parents. Through Mr. Ronald Burke's family oral history and the family research, confirmation was made that Sarah Nash Burke had a niece, Dora Nash Norton.

Dora Nash Norton migrated from Prince William, Virginia, to Alexandria. Dora's father was Sarah Nash Burke's brother. This connection would make the Norton family kin to Sarah Nash Burke, her children and the infant

Left: Ronald Burke III; *Right*: Aundrea Burke. *Courtesy the Burke family.*

Nash child who was buried at the Cemetery. The other Nash descendant will be discussed in Judy Coles Bailey's narrative.

Ronald Burke's father and mother migrated from Alexandria, Virginia, to New York. Ronald and his brother Roscoe were born in New York, while the other four siblings were born in Alexandria. Ronald's father, Robert, used to reminisce about his childhood life in Alexandria. Every summer, Ronald's parents sent him to Alexandria to be with relatives so he would experience the life that they so much cherished when they were children. Because Ronald spent so much time with his Alexandria relatives, he knew a great deal about the family history.

Ronald Burke's parents were Robert Webster Burke and Edith Russell Burke. Ronald's siblings were Robert Webster Burke Jr., Lillian Burke Maclin, Russell Hollinger Burke, Wendell Arthur Burke and Roscoe Burke. His parents and his siblings are deceased.

Mr. Ronald Burke had an adventurous life. He spent twenty years in the civil rights movement with the Southern Christian Leadership Conference (SCLC) and Operation PUSH (People United to Save Humanity) in Illinois. He worked in the manufacturing field, which afforded him the opportunity to travel and live in Nigeria, West Africa, for three years. Mr. Burke has been married to Annette Chin Burke for sixty-four years. Today, Reverend Ronald Burke Sr. is a retired Baptist minister after serving the ministry for forty years. He and his wife are enjoying their retirement in North Carolina with their two children, Ronald Burke Jr. and Robin Burke Winkfield, and their two grandchildren, Ronald Burke III and Aundrea Burke, from their son, Ronald Jr.

Mr. Ronald W. Burke and his family can now add other ancestors to their family tree who lived long enough to see their freedom.

JUDY COLES BAILEY

Armistead, Cecelia—buried February 5, 1866, age 112
Armstead, Hannah—buried February 5, 1867, age unknown, "list as old"
Harris, infant—buried February 22, 1868, age twelve hours
Harris, Julia—buried September 29, 1866, age 3

The winter of 1868 was extremely cold. Drivers on wagon carts jumped off their wagons and walked beside their horses to keep from freezing. The poor suffered greatly, including the contrabands, who did not have proper clothing and shelter. That winter of 1868 claimed the infant Harris on February 22, 1868. Previous winters, in 1866 and 1867, were less harsh when Cecelia and Hannah died.

Judy Coles Bailey and her brother, Terry Coles, heard about the Freedmen's Cemetery project and contacted the genealogist to see whether their family connected to the Freedmen's Cemetery. They knew a great deal about their family history, so this researcher confirmed what they suspected. It all began with their great-grandmother Rosa Harris Jackson Armistead. Rosa; her sister, Emma; and their mother, Mary Nash Harris, migrated from Prince William County, Virginia, to Alexandria, Virginia, during the Civil War. Mary Nash Harris had a relative in Alexandria, Sarah Nash Burke. Sarah,

Rosa Harris Jackson Armistead (1858–1951). *Courtesy Judy Coles Bailey.*

Mary and Dora Nash Norton are all from Prince William, Virginia, and they are related through Mary Nash Harris's father, Philip Nash of Prince William, Virginia. There are at least five descendant families who have been identified as descendants of the Nash family: Burke, Norton, Harris, Richards and Armstead.

Mary Nash Harris buried two children at the Freedmen's Cemetery. The Gladwin records listed all the burials at the Freedmen's Cemetery. The records showed Mary as the mother of Julia Harris, who died on September 29, 1866, and the mother of the infant Harris, who died on February 22, 1868. After the death of her two children, Mary married Sandy Hoige (Hodge) on December 28, 1869. In 1870, Sandy, Mary, Emma and Rosa were living about two houses down from Mary's relative, Sarah Nash Burke. On December 5, 1893, Mary Nash Harris Hodge died, and her husband, Sandy, died on November 27, 1896.

Jackson, boy—buried April 14, 1866, age eight

Mary's daughter, Rosa L. Harris, married her first husband, William B. Jackson, on November 18, 1880. William's mother, Millie, buried an eight-year-old boy at the Freedmen's Cemetery. After the death of William, Rosa remarried. She married William F. Armstead on November 9, 1893. William had two relatives buried at the Freedmen's Cemetery: his great-grandmother Cecelia Armistead on February 5, 1866, and his grandmother Hannah Armstead on February 5, 1867. William's mother, Celia, was named after his great-grandmother.

Rosa had several children: Richard Jackson, Mamie Jackson, Joseph Jackson, Julia Jackson, Rosa L. Armstead, Annie Armstead and Bertha Armstead. Rosa lived at 1004 Oronoco Street. She was a member of Ebenezer Baptist Church in Alexandria. Rosa was one of the first deaconesses and preachers at Ebenezer Church. She died in Alexandria on September 14, 1951. Her death certificate had her age as seventy-nine, but she was in her nineties.

Rosa Armstead Lawrence. *Courtesy Judy Coles Bailey.*

Richards, Henry—buried June 25, 1864, age one day

Rosa's sister, Emma, married Daniel C. Richard (Richards) on August 1, 1881. Daniel's parents, William Henry and Maria, buried a child, Henry Richards, on June 25, 1864, at the Freedmen's Cemetery. Emma and Daniel migrated to Philadelphia prior to 1900. Daniel died in Philadelphia on November 9, 1930, and his wife, Emma, died in Philadelphia on July 30, 1957. Emma was older than Rosa. Her death certificate had her age as ninety-nine, but she should have been over one hundred years old.

Rosa, Emma and their descendants accomplished many things that their ancestors could not have achieved. Rosa and Emma were born before the Civil War. Both of them were able to become landowners and were able to read and write. Their children, grandchildren and great-grandchildren were able to achieve their educations, secure good careers and become landowners. Rosa's daughter Rosa L. Armstead Lawrence's son, Jacob Lawrence, was a world-renowned painter of African American life. Rosa L. Lawrence's granddaughter Dr. Judy Coles Bailey pursued a career in medicine. Mary Nash Harris has many descendants in Virginia, Maryland, New Jersey, New York and Philadelphia.

NORMA JENNINGS TURNER

Butler, Margaret (twin)—buried December 2, 1864, age one day
Butler, Mary (twin)—buried December 2, 1864, age one day
Douglas, Anthony—buried March 31, 1864, age one year
Richardson, Charles—buried December 14, 1864, age sixteen years

The weather was extremely cold during the month of December 1864. A severe storm brought in hail, rain and snow. The armies were still in the area, and many of the men did not have blankets to keep themselves warm. Those troops started deserting their posts. The one-day-old Butler twins died in that miserable weather on December 2, 1864. Ten days later, another relative, Charles Richardson, died; he was sixteen years old. The twins and Charles Richardson were all buried at the Freedmen's Cemetery.

The genealogist's confidante Mrs. Norma Jennings Turner's family have been in Alexandria since the Civil War. Mrs. Turner has shared numerous stories about her family with the genealogist, including stories of her grandfather Jesse Douglass (Douglas) Speaks (Speakes). Jesse and his second wife, Mattie Hackley, have several direct and indirect family members buried at the Freedmen's Cemetery.

Jesse was named after his maternal grandfather, Jesse Douglass. Jesse Douglass was emancipated prior to 1865 in Fairfax, Virginia. He had a daughter, Lucy Douglass, who had two children prior to marrying Samuel Jackson. Lucy's daughter was Nellie Douglass, and her son was Anthony Douglass. Anthony died in 1864 and was buried at the Freedmen's Cemetery.

Jesse D. Speaks's parents were James Speaks and Rebecca Douglass. Prior to Rebecca marrying James Speaks, she married her first husband, John Butler, on January 15, 1863. Later that year, Rebecca had a daughter named Annie. About one year later, Rebecca gave birth to twins who lived for one day. Mary and Margaret were buried at the Freedmen's Cemetery on December 2, 1864.

Norma Jennings Turner.
Courtesy the author.

On December 28, 1880, Rebecca's daughter, Annie Butler, married Henry Richardson. Henry's parents were Wormley and Clarissa Richardson, who buried their oldest child, Charles, on December 14, 1864, at the Freedmen's Cemetery.

Rebecca Douglass Butler's first husband, John, died prior to 1868. On February 18, 1869, Rebecca married James Speaks in Washington, D.C. James was a veteran of the United States Colored Troops (USCT). Rebecca had seven children from her two marriages: Annie Butler, George Butler, Edwin Butler, Elizabeth Speaks, Mary K. Speaks, Jesse Speaks and William Speaks.

Prior to 1900, Rebecca Douglass Butler Speaks died. After the death of Rebecca, her three youngest children moved in with their sister Annie Butler Richardson. Rebecca's husband, James Speaks, moved to Washington, D.C. James died on June 6, 1909. Both of Rebecca's parents died prior to 1900— her mother, Mary W. Douglass, on July 24, 1893, at the age of eighty, and her father, Jesse, after 1896.

Chisley, James Henry—buried May 12, 1868, age twelve months
Chisley, Mary Dorsey—buried August 2, 1865, age three years

In 1899, Mary K. Speaks gave birth to her daughter, Annie, while she was living with her sister, Annie Richardson. In 1918, Annie married Charles H. Chisley Jr. Charles's grandparents Henry Chisley and Ann Maria Dawson migrated from Charles County, Maryland, to Alexandria, Virginia, during the Civil War. Henry Chisley's mother was Dorsey Chisley. Henry named his daughter Mary Dorsey Chisley. Mary died on August 2, 1865, at the age of three. She is buried at the Freedmen's Cemetery. Three years later, on May 12, 1868, Henry's wife, Ann Maria, buried their child James Henry Chisley. He was listed in the Gladwin burial records as being interred at St. Mary's Catholic Church cemetery, which is located across the street from the Freedmen's Cemetery.

Hackley, Gabriel—buried August 8, 1864, age fifty
Hackley, Emma—buried September 1, 1866, age one year, four months

James and Rebecca Douglass Speaks's son, Jesse D. Speaks, married his first wife, Georgia E. Lewis, prior to 1908. After the birth of their daughter, Esther, Georgia and Jesse responded to an advertisement and traveled to Salisbury, Maryland, to apply for a job at the new Peninsula General Hospital in Salisbury, which needed a cook and a porter. They were hired and worked for a least three to four years to earn enough funds to buy a home in Alexandria. Their daughter, Esther, started school in Salisbury but returned soon thereafter to Alexandria. It was difficult to purchase a home in Alexandria at that time due to the fact that one had to have most of the funds available before the purchase.

By 1920, Jesse had purchased a house at 429 North Patrick Street; his new occupation was at the shipyard as a corker. On January 8, 1926, Jesse's wife, Georgia, died. About nineteen months later, Jesse D. Speaks married Mattie L. Hackley in Washington, D.C., on September 20, 1927. Mattie's parents were James and Martha Hackley. James's father was Gabriel Hackley. Gabriel died on August 8, 1864; he is buried at the Freedmen's Cemetery. Two years later, James and Martha Hackley's daughter, Emma, died. She was buried on September 1, 1866, at the Freedmen's Cemetery.

Esther and Alexander Jennings married in 1931 and lived at 1003 Oronoco Street. Later, they purchased a home at 1019 Oronoco Street, as Alexander worked at several different careers until he was employed at the United States Post Office on Prince Street. Esther taught music lessons from their home and reared four children. Their children are Norma Jennings Turner, Doris Jennings Duncan (deceased), Jesse Alexander Jennings and Julia Jennings Caldwell.

Right: Alexander Jennings and his wife, Esther Speakes Jennings. *Courtesy Norma Jennings Turner.*

Below: *From left to right*: Howard Dishman, Norma Jennings Turner and Elizabeth Goods Brooks Evans. *Courtesy Tisara Photography.*

Mrs. Norma Turner grew up only knowing her step-grandmother, Mattie, as her grandmother. Mrs. Norma had a strong bond with her grandmother. Her grandmother was instrumental in teaching Mrs. Norma at a young age. Because her grandmother helped her, Mrs. Norma graduated from high school at the age of fifteen. Church was an important part in the life of the Speaks, Hackleys and Jennings families. Jesse D. Speaks was a member of Beulah Baptist Church, Georgia Lewis Speaks was a member of Ebenezer Baptist Church and Mattie Hackley Speaks was a member of Roberts Chapel Methodist Episcopal Church. Mrs. Norma attended church with her grandmother Mattie, and today Mrs. Norma has been at the same church for more than seventy-two years.

Three of Esther Speaks Jennings's children graduated from high school and continued their education through college and job training. Out of the four children, three followed their father, Alexander, into the federal government, and one of the children stayed home to raise her children. The children of Esther have a proud history of ancestors who were free prior to 1865; a great-grandfather, James Speaks, served in the USCT.

For this family, owning property was very important. Each generation after the Civil War became property owners. Their ancestors at the Freedmen's Cemetery have a lot to be proud of in their descendants. They continued throughout history to obtain the American dream.

DORIS (DOTTIE) WILLIAMS HUGHES

Peters, Mary—buried February 16, 1864, age one year, two months
Peters, Henry—buried January 4, 1865, age nine months

On February 16, 1864, several colored persons were baptized on this cold rainy day at the south end of Alexandria. As they were being baptized, Mary Peters was being buried. Just like Mary's funeral, Henry's funeral was on a cold day. It was not rainy, but the winds from the northwest caused the moisture to rapidly form into ice on January 4, 1865, during Henry Peters's funeral.

Mrs. Doris (Dottie) Williams Hughes heard about the Freedmen's project and asked the genealogist whether her family had any connections to the Cemetery. While interviewing Mrs. Dottie, the genealogist began gathering primary source documents: vital statistics, censuses, newspaper

Doris Williams Hughes.
Courtesy Doris Hughes.

articles, freedmen papers, property taxes, city directories, wills and cemetery records. The research revealed that Mrs. Dottie's Webster family were free before the Civil War and that her Dundas family were emancipated prior to the war. With this information, the genealogist searched the records. The genealogist discovered the not-so-obvious connection to the Freedmen's Cemetery with Mrs. Dottie's indirect ancestors, the Peters family.

The Peterses were freeborn, and so were Mrs. Dottie's Webster and Dundas families. The Dundas family were emancipated in 1837 and 1850 by the Keith family. Mrs. Dottie, through her Webster and Dundas relatives, is kin to the Peters family. The genealogist had to trace Mrs. Dottie's family back to the 1830s and then back to the twentieth century to make the connection to the Freedmen's Cemetery.

Mrs. Dottie's second great-grandparents were James Webster, born in 1814, and Letitia Edwards, born in 1818. James was a skilled carpenter. In 1880, the family lived on Alfred Street. James's wife, Letitia, died in Alexandria in 1904, and James died one year later in Massachusetts. He was visiting his daughter, Hannah Webster Hutchinson, when he died. His body was brought back to Alexandria to be buried with his wife. They are interred at the Methodist Protestant Cemetery on Wilkes Street.

Mrs. Dottie's great-grandparents Oliver Webster and Laura Dundas were married on October 11, 1872, by Pastor Thomas A. David of Roberts Chapel Methodist Episcopal Church in Alexandria. Laura Dundas Webster was named after her aunt, Laura Ann Dundas Gray. Around 1887, Oliver Webster was working for the Department of the Treasury as a laborer, making $660 per year. He was a skilled carpenter who learned this profession from his father, James Webster. In 1900, Oliver was a widower living at 120 North Peyton Street. His wife's aunt was married to William H. Gray. William had a sister, Selina Gray. She married John Peters in 1855 in Washington, D.C. Selina was born in Alexandria, and her husband, John, was born in D.C. During the Civil War, they buried two children, Mary Peters and Henry Peters, at the Freedmen's Cemetery.

Oliver Webster and his wife, Laura, had several children, and their son Samuel Webster Sr. was the grandfather of Mrs. Dottie. After 1900, Samuel married Bessie Alexander. They had about ten children. In 1930, they lived at 1109 Queen Street. Their oldest daughter, Laura Viola Webster, married Moses Harold Williams on October 17, 1929. They had five children: Doris Williams Hughes, Harold Williams, Sarah Williams Gibson, Clarice Williams Rice and Winnifred Williams Wilson. In 1940, Laura Webster Williams, her husband and children lived at 112 South Royal Street. Laura's mother, Bessie, was a widow by 1940 and was living across the street at 111 South Royal Street. Dottie and her sister Winnifred are the only living children of Moses and Laura Webster Williams.

On April 14, 1949, Doris Williams married Harry Francis Hughes. They had six children: Harry Francis Hughes Jr., Richard Oliver Hughes, Harold Steven Hughes, Michael Bob Hughes, Larry Hughes and Patrice Francine Hughes. Dottie was unaware of the rich history of her Webster and Dundas families. Dottie's third great-grandfather James Webster Sr. was Methodist. The family stayed Methodist until some of Samuel Webster Sr.'s children converted to Catholicism. Mrs. Dottie has been in the Catholic Church all her life. She is the oldest member of St. Joseph's Catholic Church in Alexandria.

The Webster family members were carpenters and butchers. They were active in their community in helping former slaves to learn to read and write. The list of their contributions in Alexandria is endless: they formed black organizations; they monitored the black education system and raised money for the early education system prior to and after 1870; they were early voters and were active in politics in Alexandria; and they were active in their church, becoming trustees in the Methodist Church. They left such a strong legacy with many contributions that their descendants are still trying to learn about.

For the two children who are buried at the Freedmen's Cemetery, they can be proud of their family's achievements.

EUGENE R. THOMPSON

Day, Betty—buried September 18, 1864, age one year
Holmes, Sarah Frances—buried April 21, 1868, age six months
Seaton, Ephraim—buried September 26, 1866, age ninety

The three people who were buried at the Freedmen's Cemetery died within four years of one another during the changing of the seasons. The

September weather for 1864 and 1866 was cool, changing from summer to fall temperatures. Unlike the weather in April 1868, when Sarah Frances Holmes died, the weather went from springlike temperatures for the month of April to winds blowing from the northwest bringing snow, hail and rain on the eve of Sarah's burial.

Eugene R. Thompson is well known in Alexandria, Virginia. He has researched his family off and on for years. This genealogist, after interviewing Eugene, concluded that he is connected to several people buried at the Freedmen's Cemetery. In addition to the interview, the author obtained many documents to confirm Eugene's connection to the Freedmen's Cemetery.

The research began with Eugene's mother, Valerie Myers Jackson Thompson. Valerie's father was Douglas Carter, and Douglas's mother was Hester Robinson Carter. Eugene and his siblings are direct descendants of Hester Robinson Carter, who is mentioned in this book under Frances Norton Burton's narrative. Valerie's mother, Mary Jackson, is indirectly related to Ruth Holmes. Ruth's grandparents Toliver (Taeaferro) and Cora had a family living in Alexandria during the Civil War. Their relatives William and

From left to right: Lillian Thompson, Eugene Thompson and Alice Thompson. *Courtesy Eugene Thompson.*

Valerie Jackson Thompson. *Courtesy Eugene Thompson.*

Caroline Holmes were living in Alexandria. William's sister, Isabella, buried her six-month-old daughter, Sarah, at the Freedmen's Cemetery. After the war, Toliver's children migrated to northern states. Some of their family now lives in Delaware.

Valerie's mother Mary Jackson's parents were Leven (Levin) and Emma Brice (Bryce) Jackson from Loudoun County, Virginia. After 1900, they migrated with their children to Alexandria. Mary's sister, Harriet A. Thompson, married Courtland Seaton in 1905. That was Courtland's second marriage. Courtland was the son of George and Catherine Seaton. The Seaton family are well known in Alexandria. They were freed African Americans prior to the Civil War; they were also builders and early politicians in Alexandria. Courtland was related to Ephraim Seaton. The former was a grandson or a great-grandson of Ephraim. Ephraim was ninety years old when he died on September 26, 1866; he is buried at the Freedmen's Cemetery. Another Seaton descendant will be discussed in Mr. James E. Henson's narrative.

Eugene's parents were Clayton Thompson and Valerie Jackson. Clayton was the son of Randolph and Mary Hamlet Thompson. Randolph's parents were Joseph and Frances (Fannie) Thompson. After 1880, Joseph Thompson and his family migrated to Alexandria from Fairfax, Virginia. Joseph's daughter, Mary Lee Thompson, married Daniel Day on November 30, 1892, in Alexandria. Daniel's parents were Thomas and Hannah Day. They were in Alexandria during the Civil War. Thomas and Hannah Day buried their child, Betty Day, at the Freedmen's Cemetery.

During the Civil War, many African American families in nearby Maryland and various counties in Virginia came to Alexandria for protection. After the war, their family members who lived in different Virginia counties and

Eugene Thompson and sister Lillian Thompson. *Courtesy Tisara Photography.*

Maryland counties migrated to Alexandria because they had families already there. The Holmes and the Jackson families were part of that migration.

The Thompson family have achieved a great deal since the Civil War. Clayton and Valerie inherited their property at 510 South Pitt Street from Clayton's parents, Randolph and Mary Hamlet, who purchased their home in 1919.

Clayton and Valerie had seven children. They became property owners, teachers and government workers. Eugene R. Thompson was the first director of the Alexandria Black History Museum in Alexandria. Lillian Thompson worked for the Alexandria School Board, and then she became an administrative assistant for Mayor William D. Euille when he was in office. Clifford Thompson worked for the United States Patent Office. William H. Thompson worked for the United States Postal Service. Gladys Thompson Turner worked for the County of Arlington. Alice Thompson Lewis retired as a teacher with thirty years of service. Clayton Thompson worked in private industry.

Eugene and his sister, Lillian, are members of Roberts Memorial United Methodist Church in Alexandria.

The Thompson family have made their mark on public service. Their descendants would be proud of their achievements.

Chapter 3

WE CAME SO FAR, JUST TO DIE

We slaves would gather around the campfire after working for twelve to fourteen hours a day. We would eat our ratios and talk about freedom. I remembered when my mother and grandmother talked about being free one day. They were sold away when I was just a little girl. Now, I got some age on me. Don't know how old I am, but I'll guess that I'm fifty years old or more. I have grown children myself, and I tell my children and grandchildren that we are going to get our freedom. They no longer laugh at me because they have been hearing about that war; we all have been hearing about the Yankees. I was born a slave, and my mama was born a slave. I even think my grandmama was born a slave. I guess my mama and grandma are with Jesus now. I prayed for them every day since they were sold away that they will meet Jesus instead of the cotton fields in the South. I want my children, my grandchildren and me to see freedom before we die. I heard the old slaves say that freedom tastes like a cold glass of water on a hot steamy day. I want my cold glass of water. Yes, I want to see freedom before I die.

There has been lots of commotion around here. We are hearing that the war has started. Old master has put on his soldier uniform, and he and all the white neighbors left on horsebacks to go fight in the war. Old mistress has been crying her eyes out asking all of us not to leave her. But I was preparing my children and grandchildren to get their belongings together because when we can steal away to get to freedom, we are going to take it.

We heard the Yankees were on the neighboring plantation. My family and I decided to make our escape following the path of the North Star. On our journey to freedom, we saw dead bodies all along the way. I quietly said a prayer for the ones who did not see freedom. They came so far just to die on the road. I prayed every step of the way that my children and grandchildren will see freedom before we die.

We met some Yankees on our way who guided us to freedom. When we crossed the army barricade to Alexandria, a safe haven for slaves, I cried so much my children thought I was sick. I cried because I was free, I cried for my mama and I cried for my grandmama because they died before they saw freedom. We prayed for freedom for so long that I just wanted to taste what freedom was like before I die.

My children and I were able to get a place to live in the barracks, and we were able to get jobs cooking and washing.

After seven months, I fell down sick. I knew that I was going to die. My children and my grandchildren gathered around me, and they were crying so much. I told them I have seen freedom before dying, and I know they are going to be okay. I looked to my right and there were my mama and grandmama stretching their hands out for me. They looked happy and they looked so good. Jesus has let me live long enough to taste that cold glass of water that the old slaves called freedom. I have come a long way, but I did not die until I tasted freedom. Mama and grandmama are waiting for me now. I have come a long way to freedom, but my children and grandchildren will live in a free world. Because of them, I will live for eternity within them.

LILLIAN LOCKLEAR ALSTON AND WANDA ELLIS

Gaines, John—buried July 28, 1864, age eight

In 1864, the month of July was extremely dry, with the water levels low, grass growing in the reservoir, the temperature very sultry and mosquitoes abounding. During this extremely hot weather, eight-year-old John Gaines was buried on July 28, 1864.

In 2008, the genealogist was informed about a potential Freedmen's Cemetery descendant. Wanda Ellis visited the Alexandria Local History/Special Collections Library to inquire about records on her ancestor. An interview between the genealogist and Wanda revealed that her family indeed was connected to the Freedmen's Cemetery. Wanda had inherited the family Bible. In the Gaines Bible was a list of marriages, births and deaths of family members. It appeared that the Bible was printed in the 1880s. Fielding Gaines, born on October 30, 1849, was the oldest birth recorded in the Bible. The genealogist researched all the information in the Bible by using federal, state and local records.

Fielding Gaines, his parents and his siblings migrated from Orange County, Virginia, to Alexandria during the Civil War. While in Alexandria,

Joseph B. Locklear with his wife, Margaret, and their children Lillian and Margaret (1943). *Courtesy Lillian Locklear Alston.*

John and Matilda Gaines (Gains) buried their eight-year-old son, John, at the Freedmen's Cemetery. Wanda Ellis is a direct descendant of John and Matilda Gaines. She is the daughter of Geraldine Ellis. Geraldine's mother, Anna Ophelia White Ellis, was married to Anderson Ellis on November 9, 1939. On Anna's marriage license, she stated that her parents were Silas White and Lucy Gaines. Lucy Gaines's death certificate states that she was

Carrie Virginia Elkins Lindsay with grandchildren Lillian E. Locklear, Grayson W. Marshall and Margaret J. Locklear (April 25, 1943). *Courtesy Lillian Locklear Alston.*

the daughter of Fielding Gaines and Ann Parker. Based on the 1870 census, Fielding Gaines was the oldest child of John and Matilda Gaines. The state and federal records matched what was in the Gaines Bible.

In 2013, an e-mail inquiry came from Lillian Locklear Alston. She noted that she was a descendant of John and Matilda Gaines. Lillian had done her own research and knew her connection to the Gaines family. John and Matilda had a daughter, Lizzie (Elizabeth), who married Horace Elkins on September 1, 1875. Horace and Lizzie migrated to Baltimore, Maryland. They had ten children; one of those children, Carrie Elkins Lindsay, was Lillian's grandmother. Carrie's daughter, Margaret Lindsay Locklear, was Lillian's mother. They are all direct descendants of John and Matilda.

Wanda Ellis had possession of the family Bible; Lillian had possession of John Gaines's property records that listed the property as "alley property" in Alexandria. She has the deed and chancery (equity) records showing that the property was paid off in three installments. The property was located parallel to North West Street and North Payne Street, the block between Queen Street and Cameron Street. John purchased this property in 1875 for sixty dollars. After 1880, Fielding, the eldest son of John and Matilda, bought property at 219 North West Street. Fielding's children and grandchildren continued to live at that property until they married or left Alexandria. This was a major achievement for John and his son, Fielding, to purchase property before the end of the nineteenth century.

Lillian and Wanda did not know each other; the genealogist made arrangements for them to meet. Both of them had pieces of their family history, but neither of them knew that their ancestor was buried at the Freedmen's Cemetery.

John and Matilda have many descendants, but at least two of their descendants continue to keep the family history alive. For Lillian Locklear

Joseph W. Alston and Lillian Locklear Alston. *Courtesy Tisara Photography.*

Alston, her children and her sister Josephine's children have built on the foundation of success started by John and Matilda. Lillian Locklear Alston retired as an assistant principal in the Baltimore City Public School System. She has an undergraduate and graduate degrees from Morgan State University. Her two daughters, Yvonne Alston and Yvette A. Gregoire, earned degrees at Carnegie Mellon University in civil engineering and at Stevens Institute of Technology, Hoboken, New Jersey, in chemical engineering. Lillian's grandsons, Phillip M. Gregoire and David A. Wicks, both have graduated from college. Lillian's sister, M. Josephine Locklear Alston, has six children. All of Josephine's children have earned college degrees, and most of them have earned advanced degrees, including two PhDs.

If the eight-year-old John had lived, he, too, would have done well. His parents, John and Matilda Gaines, laid a good foundation for their children. This foundation has lasted well over one hundred years. For the eight-year-old John Gaines, your family have done very well since the Civil War.

Dena Banks

Arrington, infant (stillborn)—buried April 21, 1868
Arrington, Nancy—buried April 27, 1866, age eleven

One week before the funeral of Nancy Arrington, it had been raining for four days, with a heavy fog covering the city. The day of Nancy's burial began with the sun peeping through the clouds.

Dena Banks contacted the genealogist back in 2008, informing her of her family's connection to the Freedmen's Cemetery. She had recognized some names on the Gladwin list of burials at the Cemetery. Emma Arrington was Dena's second great-grandmother. The Gladwin records showed Emma by name as the mother to the infant child buried at the Freedmen's Cemetery. After interviewing Dena, the genealogist searched state, federal and local records. She found that Dena is a direct descendant of the Arrington family at the Freedmen's Cemetery.

Thomas Gaskins was born around 1807, and Catharine "Katie" Arrington was born about 1812 in Prince William County, Virginia. They were a mixed-race couple who followed Katie's paternal uncle, Gayton Arrington, and his family to Alexandria, Virginia, from Prince William County, Virginia. They were escaping the Confederates during the Civil War. Thomas was a freeborn mulatto, and Katie was a white woman. They can be traced in the federal census to 1830. Although legally unable to marry, they lived together as husband and wife, having at least four children: Robert, William, Thomas and Nancy. Nancy was buried at the Freedmen's Cemetery. She appeared on the 1860 census as ten years old. At the time of her death in 1866, she was listed as eleven years old. She should have been fifteen or sixteen years old. The family's ancestral story began in three counties: Alexandria, Fairfax and Prince William, Virginia.

Dena's maternal second great-grandparents were Thomas and Katie's son, Robert Arrington, and his wife, Emily "Emma" Robinson. Emma buried her infant child at the Cemetery. Robert and Emma also had another daughter, Kate, and two sons, Thomas and Robert. After the death of Robert Sr., Emma married William Coleman and had one more child, James. In 1920, Robert Arrington Sr.'s two sons, Robert "Rhody" and Thomas Arrington, lived in Alexandria at 710 Patrick Street. Thomas Arrington and his second wife, Rhoda Thomas, are Dena's great-grandparents. Thomas's first wife, Hattie Gaines, had no children. He fathered nine children with Rhoda: five girls (Bernice, Emma Alma, Carolyn, Nancy and Almiria) and four boys

Dena Banks and her husband,
Garold Mobley. *Courtesy Dena Banks.*

(Thomas Jr., Robert, Richard and James). Bernice, born in 1922, is the only surviving child. She turns ninety-six years old in September 2018.

In the process of researching Dena's maternal side, the author made another connection to her maternal family. The Thomas and Simms families buried three people at the Freedmen's Cemetery.

Simms, Anna—buried June 29, 1865, 3 years
Simms, Frank—buried November 3, 1864, 6 months
Simms, Richard—buried October 10, 1866, no age reported

Dena's maternal grandmother, Bernice Arrington, is the granddaughter of George Thomas and Nancy Simms of Mount Vernon, Fairfax County, Virginia. Nancy's father was William Simms, son of Levi Simms and a white woman named Fannie Edmonds. William's brother, George Washington Simms, and his family migrated from the Pohick area of Fairfax, Virginia, to Alexandria, Virginia, when the Civil War started. George was interviewed by the federal government in 1871 concerning a Civil War claim. George stated that he and his family migrated at the beginning of the Civil War, as he was informed by his neighbor's slave that his white neighbors were going to capture him and his family. The neighbors were planning to sell them down south. George and his family were free people of color. He gathered his family and fled to Alexandria, leaving the cooking pot under the fire in the middle of the yard. George worked for the Union for a short time as a blacksmith during the war. He and his family stayed in Alexandria for several years after the Civil War. George lived at and ran his blacksmith business at an alley dwelling on Gibbon Street. While in Alexandria, he and his wife buried three children at the Freedmen's Cemetery.

The early Arrington and the Simms families were mixed-race people who married white women. These mixed families challenged the racial laws of the times that outlawed racial cohabitation. The two families were entrepreneurs and landowners. Thomas Arrington was born in 1869, the son of Robert Arrington. Thomas owned his store in Alexandria. George Washington Simms, who was born in 1813, was a blacksmith and a politician. He was selected for the grand jury for the treason trial of the president of the Confederacy, Jefferson Davis. (President Davis was never tried.)

Just like Dena's maternal side, her paternal side were also entrepreneurs. Today, Dena continues her family's legacy. She is the daughter of Olander Banks Jr. and Rhoda Evans Forrest. Her mother graduated from Luther Jackson High School in Merrifield, Virginia. Rhoda also attended college and graduated from Federal City College in Washington, D.C. Dena's father, Olander Jr., graduated from Parker-Gray High School in Alexandria. After high school, Olander worked for his father in the family business, Banks Auto Parts Inc., which started in Alexandria, and he owned his own trucking business, Banks Trucking. Dena has two siblings, Angela Banks Queen and Olander Banks III. Dena and her husband, Garold Mobley, own Mosaic Barber & Beauty Salon. They have two locations in Prince William County, Virginia. They have a combined family of eight children—four boys and four girls—and four grandchildren.

The Arrington and Simms families have really made their mark in Alexandria, Fairfax and Prince William, Virginia. They were skilled workers and business owners, served in the military, were early property owners and were college educated. They were determined to take control of their destiny. Their ancestors should be proud that they have achieved so much prior and after the Civil War.

Lois Diggs Davis and Richard Diggs

Diggs, Cesar—buried August 8, 1866, age twenty-three
Diggs, Fanny—buried August 8, 1864, age twenty-nine
Diggs, infant—buried August 7, 1864, age one day
Diggs, Husten—buried July 8, 1864, age six

The first part of August 1864 had lightning and thunder, with heavy rains flooding the area. By morning, the rain had stopped, and the early morning temperatures were just as hot as the evening temperatures. Fanny gave birth on August 6, and her infant child died the next day on August 7, 1864. Fannie also joined her infant child on August 8, 1864.

Irene Gaskins Macklin introduced this author to Lois Diggs Davis. In the process of interviewing Lois and her brother, Fredrick Diggs, the genealogist learned about another Diggs relative who connected to Lois's family going back to the 1850s. Among these two Diggs family members, Lois and Richard, four Diggs family members were buried at the Freedmen's Cemetery.

Lois's second great-grandparents were William and Nancy Diggs. William was born around 1821. Although William is documented in Alexandria in 1863, it is possible that he might have been in Alexandria much earlier. Based on the 1865 *Alexandria Real and Personal Property Taxes Paid by African Americans*, William paid fifty dollars property tax on a house in Ward 3. William Diggs's sister, Fannie, and her infant child are buried at the Freedmen's Cemetery. William named his daughter Fannie after his sister. Also, William had another child, Husten Diggs, who is buried at the Freedmen's Cemetery.

Richard Diggs's second great-grandparents were Richard and Rebecca Butt Diggs. Richard's family line can be documented in Alexandria to

From left to right: Lois Diggs Davis, Shannon Quarles and Michael Diggs. *Courtesy Tisara Photography.*

1850. Richard's third great-grandfather Richard was born in 1830. For Richard and Lois, both of their families are related to one another. Lois's father, Julian, born in 1899, claimed that he was related to Richard Diggs's family. Richard and his wife, Rebecca, were on the 1860 census. Richard's younger brother, Cesar Diggs, was buried at the Freedmen's Cemetery on August 8, 1866.

Lois's father Julian's maternal side also buried a child at the Freedmen's Cemetery.

Scott, Courtney—buried January 13, age one day

Julian's mother was Mary Scott Diggs. Her parents were Morris (Maurice) Scott and Martha Lacy. He was born in Louisa, Virginia, and she was born in Fauquier, Virginia. The genealogist identified Courtney Scott, who is buried at the Freedmen's Cemetery, as Morris and Martha's child. The clue to Courtney's parents was in the 1870 census of Alexandria. Morris and Martha lived in the household of Courtney Landon in Alexandria. They named their firstborn child after Courtney Landon. Shortly after the 1870 census, Morris and his wife moved to her hometown in Fauquier, Virginia. They were back in Alexandria before 1875. Morris lived on Prince Street. By 1880, Morris and Martha had four children: Willie, Robert, Mary and Connie. Morris worked for the railroad. In 1910, Morris lived at 1211 Cameron Street; he was a widow. His daughter, Mary Morris Scott and her two children, William and Julian, lived with him.

Lois Diggs and Richard Diggs have followed in their ancestors' footsteps by having good careers and establishing their own business. Lois was a director of corporate sponsorship and conventions with the National Community Pharmacist Association in Alexandria. She has three sons, Kevin, Gregory and Richard Quarles, and one daughter, Michelle Quarles. She has twelve grandchildren and six great-grandchildren. Her siblings are Thomas, Fredrick (deceased), Irving, William (deceased), Richard, Michael, David (deceased), Norman Shanklin (deceased), Julian (deceased), James Diggs (deceased), John Diggs (deceased) and Mary Goodsby (deceased). Lois Diggs's family members were early members of Third Baptist Church. Today, Lois and her family are members of Oakland Baptist Church in Alexandria.

Richard Diggs's family members were entrepreneurs and educators. Richard is president and CEO of Alexandria Pest Services, Springfield, Virginia. He graduated from T.C. Williams High School in 1972. His parents

Frederick L. Diggs (*left*) and Richard Diggs. *Courtesy Tisara Photography.*

are Lloyd Diggs and Barbara Scott. Richard has two children, Richard and Jasmine. He also has two grandchildren. Richard's siblings are Grace Diggs Coates, Lloyd Diggs, Hope Diggs Mayfield, Adrienne Diggs Lee and Steven Diggs (deceased). Richard Diggs's family members were early members of Shiloh Baptist Church in Alexandria. Today, Richard is a member of Woodlawn Faith Methodist Church.

Throughout the history of the Diggs and Scott families, their given names have been repeated with every generation. Richard Diggs was born in 1830 and William Scott in 1840. Their families were proud, hardworking people. They were well respected in their community, and their name carried weight. The descendants are proud to continue to carry the family's name.

HOWARD DISHMAN AND LYNNWOOD CAMPBELL

Addison, Mina—buried February 1, 1864, age fourteen

The last week of January 1864 was mild and slightly windy, but on the last day of the month, the weather turned wintery cold, with drizzle and chilly winds, all coming from the northeast. That weather was the same on February 1, 1864, during which fourteen-year-old Mina Addison was buried.

The author knows Mr. Howard Dishman Sr. and his wife, Dana, and has interviewed him several times over the last ten years. He has a long history in Alexandria, Virginia.

Howard's maternal grandparents were Frederick R. Howard and Cora Bentley. They were married in 1907. His grandfather Frederick was the son of Alexander Howard and Sarah Addison. Sarah stated in her marriage license that her parents were Frederick and Louise. The fourteen-year-old child Mina Addison was Frederick and Louise's daughter; she was buried on February 1, 1864, at the Freedmen's Cemetery. Sometime around 1870, Frederick Addison died; his wife, Louise lived on Queen Street with her children, including her daughter, Sarah, who was eight years old.

Inez Howard Dishman and son Howard Dishman Sr. *Courtesy Howard Dishman Sr.*

Mr. Howard Dishman also has relatives on his maternal grandmother's side who are buried at the Freedmen's Cemetery.

Craig, Ellen—buried October 9, 1864, age twenty-five
Craig, Emily—buried August 11, 1865, age eighteen
Craig, William—buried May 1, 1864, age thirty

Dorothea Bentley Campbell; her son, Lynnwood Campbell; Howard Dishman; and their families are the descendants of Ellen, Emily and William Craig and are buried at the Freedmen's Cemetery. Dorothea and Howard are second cousins. Dorothea's father, Louis Bentley, and Howard's grandmother Cora Bentley Howard Banks are siblings. Louis and Cora's mother Susan Craig Bentley's parents were William and Jane. Jane's husband, William, is buried at the Freedmen's Cemetery. Also Jane's two in-laws, Ellen and Emily Craig, are buried at the Freedmen's Cemetery. The genealogist found a lot of discrepancies with Jane Craig Alexander's age and previous marital status, but after some research, the full story of Jane emerged. Jane married

Left: Lynnwood Campbell and Dorothea G. Campbell. *Courtesy Lynnwood Campbell.*

Right: Richard Bentley (1853–1939). *Courtesy Howard Dishman.*

her second husband, Samuel Alexander, on June 16, 1870, in Alexandria. Her date of birth is between the years 1820 and 1830, and her age was incorrect on her second marriage license. Also, Jane's daughter Susan Craig Bentley's marriage license stated that Samuel and Jane were her parents. Susan was a little girl when her father, William, died. A later document stated that Susan's father was William. The Craig family were from Fauquier County, Virginia. Susan and Mary Craig were confirmed as the children of William and Jane Craig. Both of the children were born in Loudoun County, Virginia, before William and Jane migrated to Alexandria during the Civil War. In 1900, Jane lived in the household of her son-in-law, Richard Bentley, and her daughter, Susan, at 315 North Patrick Street.

Susan Craig Bentley's husband, Richard, was a successful property owner. Prior to 1870, he started buying property in Alexandria. The property at 315 North Patrick Street has been in the Bentley's family for 150 years. Richard also owned several parcels of land in the 300 block of North Patrick Street. When his children became adults, he gave them some property. In his lifetime, he became a store owner and storekeeper and had a business in

Howard Dishman receiving roses at the dedication ceremony. *Courtesy Tisara Photography.*

wood and coal. When he was younger, he was a waiter and a laborer at the Potomac Yards. Richard's great-grandson Howard Dishman, granddaughter Inez and daughter Cora inherited his house at 315 North Patrick Street. That house was passed down to Mr. Howard Dishman. Today, Mr. Dishman and his wife, Dana, live in the family's home.

Howard is the son of Howard A. Dishman and Inez Howard. He spent two years in the navy, and he retired after thirty-five years as a dry cleaner and manager. He has two children, Beverly Dishman Tremble and Howard Dishman Jr. (deceased). He also is a grandfather of three and a great-grandfather of two. He and his second wife, Dana, have been married since 2006. They are members of Meade Memorial Episcopal Church. Howard's mother was also a member of Meade Memorial Episcopal Church. His grandmother Cora Bentley Howard Banks was a member of Third Baptist Church.

Dorothea Bentley Campbell and her two sisters, Theresa Bentley Carter and Frankie Bentley Lyles, are the last surviving grandchildren of Susan Craig Bentley. On May 10, 1946, Dorothea married Lynnwood Campbell

From left to right: Lynnwood Campbell, Dana Dishman and Howard Dishman. *Courtesy Tisara Photography.*

upon his return from World War II as a Marine Corps veteran. Dorothea lived at 313 North Patrick Street, next door to her grandfather's house at 315 North Patrick Street. Lynnwood Campbell Sr. lived at 309 North Patrick Street. Dorothea had a long career as a beautician. She and her husband had four children: Wilma Campbell Anderson (deceased), Lynnwood Campbell Jr., Zachary Moore and Bernard Campbell. Her son Lynnwood Jr. is a college graduate from Howard University. He served in the army as a captain in the Finance Corps. He has an outstanding career as a certified public accountant, working in the private sector and the federal government. He was a former vice-chairman of the Alexandria Public School Board and former chairman of the United Way of the National Capital Area. In 2011, Lynnwood Jr. became an Alexandria's Living Legend. He is married to his high school sweetheart, Deborah Sandra Hill. They have one daughter, Robin Campbell. Lynnwood is a life member of St. Joseph's Catholic Church. He also attended St. Joseph's Catholic Elementary School, and he was the first African American to attend and graduate from St. Mary's Elementary School in 1961.

Richard Bentley set a high bar for his descendants. He was a hardworking person, and he earned his wealth in real estate. His descendants have added on to Richard's legacy. For their Addison and Craig families buried at the Freedmen's Cemetery, they should be proud that their struggle for freedom did not go in vain. The descendants have achieved more than they could have dreamed of. They are proud to be part of this family.

ROSALIND DRAYTON LANFORD AND EUGENE S. DRAYTON JR.

Drayton, infant—buried November 19, 1866, no age given

Just a few days before the death of the infant, you could hear geese passing over the city on their way to southern latitudes. This was always a sign that cold weather was coming. Before winter weather started, the Drayton child had been buried on November 19, 1866, at the Freedmen's Cemetery.

The genealogist found the Drayton descendants by using school records from the former segregated Parker-Gray High School, operated from 1920 to 1965. In those records, Eugene Shanklin Drayton Jr. was in the graduating class of 1957. With Eugene's assistance, he introduced his family to the researcher. His cousin Sharon Dunlop Green and his uncle, Bertram D. Drayton, were helpful in confirming their family history. Through research, the genealogist determined that the Drayton family were the only African American Draytons living in Alexandria during the Civil War.

Bertram D. Drayton (1926–2014). *Courtesy the author.*

Joyce Sanders (*left*), Ethel Drayton (*sitting center*), Eugene S. Drayton Jr. (*upper left*), Irving L. Drayton (*upper center*) and Elaine Burton (*lower left*). *Courtesy Eugene S. Drayton Jr.*

During the war, their ancestor Harrison Drayton migrated to Alexandria, Virginia, from Massachusetts. Based on research, the genealogist believed that Harrison might have been part of the United States Colored Troops, but documentation was not available to confirm his military service. But what is known is that Harrison and his wife, Emma, buried an infant child at the Freedmen's Cemetery. Emma was recorded in the Gladwin burial records as the mother of the infant child who died November 19, 1866.

Bertram D. Drayton is the great-grandson of Harrison and Emma Drayton. Bertram's parents were Charles Harrison Drayton Sr. and Irene Shanklin. Eugene's parents are Eugene S. Drayton Sr. and Ethel Dial. Sharon Dunlop Green's parents are George L. Dunlop and Mary Ellen Drayton. This Drayton family also connects to the Shanklin family.

Shanklin, Berkey—buried March 9, 1864, age ninety
Shanklin, child—buried December 12, 1865, no age given

During the Civil War, there were two different Shanklin families living in Alexandria. Those Shanklins were not related to each other. But both of those Shanklin families buried family members at the Freedmen's Cemetery. The Draytons' Shanklin family were in Alexandria prior to the Civil War.

On December 19, 1863, James Shanclin (Shanklin) married Maria Roberts. James stated that his parents were Bartley (Berkley) and Margaret. On March 9, 1864, James's father, Berkley, was buried at the Freedmen's Cemetery. One year later, Maria was listed in the Gladwin records burying an infant child on December 12, 1865. After the death of Maria, James married Ella Henshaw. Ella Henshaw Shanklin was Bertram Drayton's maternal grandmother.

Strange, Nelson—buried April 26, 1864, age fifty

On June 28, 1947, Bertram D. Drayton married Ruth Harriet Strange. Bertram lived at his parents' home at 416 Oronoco Street, and Ruth lived at her parents' home at 607 South Columbus Street. Her parents were Richard Emmanuel Strange and Margaret Lyles. Ruth's second great-grandfather Reverend Jacklyn Strange, who was born free in 1837, became a well-known Methodist minister at Roberts Chapel Methodist Episcopal Church in Alexandria.

In 1858, Jacklyn (Jacquelin) Strange lived in Alexandria, Virginia, and he registered in the courthouse as a freeborn black person. On May 29, 1862, Jacklyn married Hannah Weaver. He was born in Winchester, Virginia, and Hannah was born in Alexandria. They were married by a Methodist clergyman, C.A. Reid of Trinity Methodist Episcopal Church, the mother church of Roberts Chapel Methodist Episcopal Church.

During the Civil War, Jacklyn's relative Nelson Strange migrated from Fauquier, Virginia, to Alexandria. On April 26, 1864, Nelson Strange died; he is buried at the Freedmen's Cemetery. Bertram's daughter Rosalind Drayton Lanford's maternal second great-grandparents were Jacklyn and Hannah Strange. Hannah was a member of Alfred Street Baptist Church. They lived walking distance from Alfred Street Baptist Church at 807 Duke Street. On January 5, 1917, Hannah Strange was at home sick when Reverend Powell from Alfred Street Baptist Church visited her. Mrs. Strange had a conversation with the reverend about how she wanted her funeral arranged, and hours later, she died. Reverend Jacklyn Strange outlived his wife by five years. He died on February 20, 1922. Rosalind is a direct descendant of Reverend Jacklyn Strange. On July 16, 2014, Bertrum D. Drayton died; he was a World War II veteran. He is buried at the Maryland Veterans Cemetery in Prince George's County.

The family have continued to progress financially. Harrison Drayton in 1870 lived at Fayette near Princess Street. He was a laborer for the City of

Alexandria but later became a store owner. Other family members had jobs in the federal government, state government, military services and private companies.

As for Eugene S. Drayton Jr., he retired as a law librarian for the Los Angeles County Council. After completing high school in 1957, he entered the United States Air Force. After completing his military service, he moved to Los Angeles and attended the University of California, Los Angeles (UCLA), receiving his undergraduate degree in 1972. In 1973, he attended the University of Southern California and received a master's degree in library science.

The surnames Drayton, Shanklin and Strange are not familiar names in Alexandria's early history. These surnames appeared in Alexandria through migration as early as the late 1850s by black families who were fleeing from the onset of the Civil War. Because those surnames were not common, they stood out from other common names of families who migrated to Alexandria. Once you found one family member, you were able to connect to other relatives in the area.

For your ancestors who are buried at the Freedmen's Cemetery even after 150 years, your family members are still in the Alexandria area. They have maintained the family history and are chasing the American dream.

Chapter 4

FREEDOM DIDN'T
COME EASY

Child let me tell you about our freedom. It did not come easy. We remembered those slave days like it was yesterday. When we were little children, we heard the adults talking about Nat Turner—that old Nat is coming to free us all, they would said. Mama said I wasn't even born when old Nat went crazy. She said they were all praying that freedom would come. Nat got caught and killed; many slaves thought that his spirit would return to free us. Mama said things got really bad on the plantations after Nat died. All the masters on the plantations were afraid that we were some of Nat's folks, waiting to kill them. So they started putting more restrictions on the slaves. We had to be in our cabins by a certain time. We couldn't stand around talking to the other slaves without the overseer lashing us. Even our food rations were cut. We were always hungry. Sometimes I think that the masters and the mistresses are afraid that the pain they caused us will one day come to them. If they could only feel our pain, maybe, just maybe, they will let us go free.

Mama said that Dad was a runaway. He wanted freedom, so one night he ran toward the North Star. After three months, Mama said they knew he made it north. They said usually you get caught within a month or so. So all the slaves on the plantation knew Daddy made it north.

About three weeks later, we were working in the fields when we heard the overseer telling us to go into the yard. "Now!" he said. We did not know what was going on. All thirteen of us gathered in the front yard, and we saw them drag this man out of the barn. He had deep gashes on his back, and blood was gushing. His face was blistered and swollen. I heard my Mama make a noise that I have never heard before. The slaves were whispering saying that it looks like Big Jack—that is Big Jack! We children gave that man a hard look, and we could see part of his face—it looked like him. It was Daddy! Lord, they had striped him down to his waist and beat him over and over again. The overseer kept repeating his words, telling Big Jack, "You will never run away. You will never run away again. You will never get your freedom as long as I live." The overseer took the hoe and smashed my Dad's foot. Then he took a bucket of salty water and threw all that water on my Daddy's wounds. My Daddy passed out. No one moved to help him. They were all afraid. After several hours, the overseer told some of the male slaves to take Big Jack in the barn and dress his wounds. The overseer told Big Jack, "You rest tomorrow but you're back to work after that." No one said a word about what we saw. Mama cried that night, cried for Daddy and cried for us. She said none of us should talk about freedom. She said, "If I see any of my babies beaten like Big Jack, I will just die."

Daddy came back to the cabin, and Mama nursed his wounds day after day. Every day, he went to the fields, working harder than before. After five years, we started hearing about the war. We heard that the war had started. Mama's mother worked in the Big House. She told Daddy that freedom was coming. Daddy told Mama that they will have to take a chance and get their freedom. Mama was so afraid, she started rocking back and forth. She said, "Big Jack, if we run and get caught they will kill you and sell us."

Big Jack turned around and held Mama by her shoulders and said, "Woman! We are gonna die if we stay, or we gonna die trying to be free, or we gonna to die in freedom, but we are not staying here."

Grandma said to Big Jack, "We should wait for the Yankees to come and then we will travel with the Yankees." Well, a month later, the Yankees came to the plantation. We started praying and thanking God all over the place. Dad wiped the tears from his eyes. He asked the Yankees if we can travel with them. Yankees said that we can help with the cooking and washing, and Dad can work on odd jobs that they might have. They allowed all of us to join them. Old master and the mistress stood in the doorway of the Big House, looking like death has come their way. As we packed our small belongings, we heard the master say, "This is your home, you can stay."

My Daddy, my Mama and all of us walked out of the cabin carrying our small bags, lining up behind the Yankees. As we were leaving, Daddy took a good look at the overseer, who was standing near the opening gates to the plantation. Daddy said, "Freedom, Oh, Freedom!" Freedom wasn't easy, but it was sweet when it came.

Joyce Paige Anderson Abney

Gibson, child—buried August 2, 1868, no age given
Gibson, Hannah—buried May 27, 1865, age eighty-five

May 1865 had days of mixed weather. By the second week of the month, the weather turned cool and hail was falling, covering the neighborhood with large hailstones. By the third week of May, spring was back again with showers. On May 27, 1865, Hannah was buried as the spring flowers were blooming.

The genealogist met Mrs. Joyce Paige Anderson Abney over thirty-five years ago in college in Washington, D.C. They found out that both of them are native Alexandrians. Joyce always talked about her family and what life was like growing up in Alexandria. So when the genealogist began working on the Freedmen's project, Joyce was one of the first people to be interviewed. Joyce's parents were Gertrude Paige and Charles Butler. Her paternal grandmother was Dorothy Gibson. Mrs. Abney was a devoted granddaughter. She spent a lot of time with her grandparents, learning about their history and the history of the people who lived around them. Joyce's family connected to the Freedmen's Cemetery on several lines.

Joyce's grandmother Dorothy Gibson's family were in Alexandria during the Civil War. Dorothy's great-grandparents Henry Gibson and Lucy Ann Graves were married on February 2, 1865, in Alexandria, Virginia. This was Henry's second marriage. He was born in Warrenton, Virginia, and his wife, Lucy, was born in Stafford, Virginia. His parents were Christopher and Hannah. Henry and his wife were married by Reverend George W. Parker at Third Baptist Church. Three months after Henry got married, his eighty-five-year-old mother died and was buried at the Freedmen's Cemetery. Henry and Lucy were living on the corner of Pitt and Pendleton Street when their infant child died on August 2, 1868. In 1880, Henry and his wife lived at 393 North

From left to right: Donna Anderson, Joyce Paige Anderson Abney, Robin Anderson and Robert Anderson. *Courtesy Joyce Paige Anderson Abney.*

Alma Paige. *Courtesy Joyce Paige Anderson Abney.*

Pitt Street. They had two children, Maria and Daniel. Henry's occupation was a railroad hand; he had been with the railroad for more than ten years. Henry and Lucy's son, Daniel, married Louise Hollins (Holland) on March 8, 1899. Daniel's father, Henry, was already deceased by 1899. Another family member who is indirectly connected to Joyce Anderson Abney was buried at the Freedmen's Cemetery.

Kier, Jannie—buried October 7, 1868, age two

In 1886, Daniel's widow mother, Lucy Graves Gibson, remarried. On July 5, 1886, Lucy Gibson married Marshall Kyer (Kier). Marshall was a sixty-one-year-old widow. He was born in 1825 in Fauquier, Virginia; Marshall lived in Alexandria during the Civil War. On October 7, 1868, Marshall and his first wife, Lucetta, buried their two-year-old child, Jannie Kier (Kyer), at the Freedmen's Cemetery. After the death of Daniel, Lucy's daughter-in-law, Louise Holland Gibson, remarried. She married Marshall Kyer's son, William Kyer. They lived at 513 North Pitt Street. William died on June 5, 1917. His funeral was at Third Baptist Church.

Webster, Martin—buried February 10, 1865, age twelve

Another one of Joyce's ancestors buried a child at the Freedmen's Cemetery. Elizabeth Fairfax Webster Ward was the mother of Joyce's great-grandfather William Henry Webster. Elizabeth, sometimes known as Lizzie, kept an 1884 family Bible that has stayed in the family, and Joyce is now the keeper of that Bible, which lists the connection to the different family lines. It is believed that William H. Webster's father, Armistead Webster, buried Martin Webster on February 10, 1865, at the Freedmen's Cemetery.

Joyce Paige Anderson Abney had two siblings, William L. Paige (deceased) and Evelyn V. Butler Jones. Joyce is an exceptional woman. She raised four children and attended college part-time for more than a decade to complete her two undergraduate degrees in computer science technology and elementary education. Joyce retired from the Washington, D.C., Public School System with thirty-five and a half years of service. In 1957, Joyce married Robert G. Anderson. They had four children: Robert, Robin, Donna and Theresa. She also has thirteen grandchildren and five great-grandchildren. Joyce remarried in 1993 to Ervin H. Abney, who is now deceased.

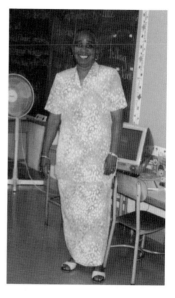

Joyce Paige Anderson Abney. *Courtesy Joyce Abney.*

It is not surprising to Joyce's ancestors that she is a fighter. Joyce has fought all her life to obtain the American dream for herself and family. Joyce knew that the strength of her ancestors gave her the courage to endure the many obstacles in pursuing her life's dream. The ancestors are proud that she has achieved her dream and has added another milestone to their family legacy.

LATOSHA JACKSON, GERALD WANZER, LUCIAN JOHNSON AND FRANCES COLBERT TERRELL

Jackson, Andrew—buried August 6, 1864, age one year, three months

In the late summer of 1864, the weather was extremely hot with no rain in sight, which made the heat unbearable for the young, the old and the sick. On August 6, 1864, Andrew Jackson was buried during that miserably hot weather.

The author met Latosha Jackson after the death of her father, William Jackson. Prior to the death of William Jackson, he and his siblings Jean, George and Harold were identified as descendants of the Freedmen's Cemetery. William Jackson was the grandson of Robert Jackson and Mary Wanzer Jackson Hall. His great-grandparents were James Jackson and Catharine (Kitty) Brooks. They were married on April 24, 1866. James was born in 1845 to Andrew Jackson and Maria Martin. Andrew and Maria buried their son, Andrew Jackson, on August 6, 1864, at the Freedmen's Cemetery. They had two more children after Andrew; unfortunately, those children died before they were three years old.

Latosha, Charmeise Rajon and Natressa Jackson are also descendants of the Wanzer family through their great-grandmother Mary Wanzer-Jackson Hall.

From left to right: Latosha Jackson, Harold Jackson and Jean Jackson. The family of William Jackson. *Courtesy Tisara Photography.*

Wanser, infant—buried June 3, 1866, age two days
Wanzer, Betsey—buried June 23, 1865, age fifteen
Wanzer, Catharine—buried January 6, 1865, no age given
Wanzer, Lucy—buried August 7, 1863, age eight

The Wanzer (Wanser) family are well known in Alexandria. During the Civil War, they lived in Alexandria in the Jefferson District until 1880. There were several Wanzer families in Alexandria, under Wallace Wanzer, George Wanzer, Marshall Wanzer and John Wanzer. Those Wanzers are believed to be related to one another. Based on their ages, they were probably siblings. What has been confirmed is that the two-day-old Wanser infant buried on June 3, 1866, was George Wanser's child. On January 6, 1865, Catharine Wanzer was buried at the Freedmen's Cemetery. She was confirmed as the child of Wallace and Jennie (Virginia) Wanzer. The other two children, Lucy and Betsey Wanzer, are buried at the Freedmen's Cemetery; their parents have not been confirmed. They are related to the Wanzers. Most of the Wanzers who came to Alexandra were born in Fauquier County, Virginia, and one of them was born in Stafford, Virginia.

All of the descendants who have been located for the Wanzer family are descendants of Wallace Wanzer, who was born around 1835. Wallace was in Alexandria as early as 1857. The author researched each one of his children, and all of them were born in Alexandria or Fairfax, Virginia. That places Wallace and his wife, Jennie, in Alexandria several years before the Civil War.

Wallace was a skilled blacksmith and wheelwright. In the 1880s, Wallace purchased property in the west end of Alexandria. On July 21, 1910, Wallace died at his home. The *Washington Post* newspaper reported on July 22, 1910, that "Wallace Wanzer, a well-known and respected colored blacksmith, died yesterday at his home near the Episcopal Theological Seminary in Fairfax County, Virginia."

Wallace and Jennie (Virginia) had at least fifteen children. Out of the fifteen children, Mary Wanzer Jackson Hall, Joseph Wanzer and Alice Wanzer Simms's descendants have been found.

The Wanzer family have continued Wallace Wanzer's legacy in working hard and purchasing property. The early Wanzers established a long relationship with the Episcopal Theological Seminary. Many of the Wanzers worked at the seminary over the generations. Other family members have accomplished careers in the military, federal and state government and as firefighter, air traffic controller and public officials; some have obtained higher degrees at universities.

Fannie Wanzer. *Courtesy Gerald Wanzer.*

Left: Daniel and Viola Wanzer. *Courtesy Gerald Wanzer.*

Right: Clifton Wanzer (*left*) and Gerald Wanzer (*right*:). *Courtesy Tisara Photography.*

Joseph Wanzer's son, Daniel Wanzer, was a postal employee. He retired from the post office located on Washington Street in Alexandria. Daniel Wanzer and his wife, Viola, had six children. Clifton, Janet Wanzer Golden and Gerald are Daniel's surviving children. Clifton Wanzer retired as an air traffic controller with thirty-eight years in aviation. He also spent four years in the air force. Gerald Wanzer also enlisted in the air force. He was in the service from 1963 to 1967. After his military career, he worked for the C&P Telephone Company as an installer/repairman, and after two years with the telephone company, he landed the job of his dream. He became a fireman at the Alexandria Fire Department in 1969. Due to a job injury, he was forced to retire.

Wallace Wanzer's daughter, Mary Wanzer Jackson Hall, had just as many children as her parents—seventeen in all. Her son Preston Hall was on the Advisory Neighborhood Commission in Washington, D.C., a traffic management specialist for the federal government and a minister. Her son Dr. Elisha G. Hall was an assistant mayor in Charlottesville, Virginia; president of Virginia University of Lynchburg, Virginia; and a Baptist minister for forty-five years. Two of her sons, Matthew Hall and Nathaniel Hall, lived in New York. Both of them had their own business. Her daughter Dorothy Beatrice Hall Smith is a college graduate with a master's degree in public administration/urban society.

Delaney and Mary Agnes Johnson Colbert. *Courtesy Frances Colbert Terrell.*

Terrell and Wanzer family. *Courtesy Tisara Photography.*

Another one of Wallace's daughters Alice Wanzer Simms's descendants made their contributions to their family legacy. Her grandson Lucian Johnson also had a military career. When he completed his military service, he obtained a job with the federal government. Just like his great-grandfather, he purchased his home. Alice's great-granddaughter Frances Colbert Clements Terrell worked for the federal government. She spent twenty-three of her thirty years of service as a Congressional staffer for the United States House of Representatives. She is also a homeowner.

Wallace Wanzer has been very successful. He was a highly skilled blacksmith and repaired wagon wheels, owned his own property, witnessed the building of Oakland Baptist Church and had the respect of his community. Today, many of his descendants are members of Oakland Baptist Church.

Wallace Wanzer and his ancestors have a lot to be proud of. Their descendants have continued to claim their American dream.

Bernice Robinson Lee

Lumpkin, Delila—buried October 19, 1866, age two

Five days before Delila (Delilah) Lumpkin died, a heavy storm hit the city of Alexandria, causing the Alexandria Canal banks to overflow, which damaged the railroad station and washed out roadways. On October 19, 1866, the weather had changed. Delilah died on a nice autumn day.

Mrs. Bernice Robinson Lee's Lumpkins family are well known in Alexandria. Her mother, Mrs. Helen Lumpkins Robinson Day, was also a well-known twentieth-century teacher, who made an impact on many people in Alexandria. Her family were the only African American family in Alexandria who had the surname Lumpkins during the Civil War. Mrs. Lee's great-grandparents were Gustavus (Gus) A. Lumpkins and Catharine Buckner.

Based on the oral history of the Lumpkins family, Gus, his wife and their oldest son, Patrick, were enslaved before the war. During slavery, Patrick's mother had to tie him to her waist to work in the fields, and that caused the young Patrick to have paralysis in his right hand. He learned to write with his left hand. During the Civil War, they migrated from Loudoun to Alexandria, where they found refuge until the war ended.

After Alexandria emancipated its slaves on April 7, 1864, Gus and his family made progress. However, that progress was short-lived. They

Patrick H. Lumpkins (1856–1919).
*Courtesy Alexandria Library, Special
Collections, Alexandria, Virginia.*

faced setbacks when their daughter, Delilah Lumpkin, died in 1866. She was buried at the Freedmen's Cemetery. In 1875, Gus was the proprietor of Fountain House (boardinghouse) at 179 King Street; he also had a shoe business at 135 Cameron Street. In 1897, Gus and his family moved to 810 Queen Street, and his occupation was listed as shoemaker. After the death of Catharine, Gus lived with his youngest son, James, and his wife in 1900. Gustavus A. Lumpkins died before 1910.

His descendants made an enormous impact on the African American community during their lifetime. Gus and Catharine had two sons, Patrick and James. James was born in Alexandria, Virginia, in 1868; he attended Howard University and graduated with a two-year certificate. James became a United States postal clerk in Washington, D.C.

Patrick was born in 1854 in Loudoun, Virginia. He attended school at Howard University but left college before completing the program. He began teaching in the Virginia school system around 1885. He was a member of Roberts Chapel Methodist Episcopal Church in Alexandria and a contributor to the church music programs for more than forty years. He helped to increase membership in the church through his music. He sang in the church choir in the 1870s, directed the church music programs and organized the Epworth League Choir and the Brotherhood Choir. He served as superintendent of Sunday school.

In 1897, Patrick gave a musical performance that was the talk of the town, and the famous Booker T. Washington attended Roberts Chapel Methodist Episcopal Church on his visit to Alexandria. Mr. Lumpkins was also active in his community affairs. He connected to the young as well as the old. On September 15, 1919, he died at his home on 615 South Columbus Street. Patrick and his wife, Lucy, had two children, Helen and Patrick Jr.

Helen Lumpkins Robinson Day followed in her father's footsteps as a teacher; she influenced more people than her father. She was an organist and a junior choir director for Roberts Chapel Methodist Church for twenty-nine years. She graduated from Miner Teachers College in Washington,

From left to right: Bernice Robinson Lee, Lucy Washington with baby Carol Lee and Helen Day. *Courtesy Alexandria Black History Museum.*

D.C., and then taught at Parker-Gray School and at Charles Houston Elementary School in Alexandria for more than forty-four years. She was a leader in social, cultural, educational and political organizations. Two institutions are named after Mrs. Helen Day: the Hopkins House—Helen Day Preschool Academy and the Helen Day United States Post Office Building in Alexandria.

Mrs. Helen Day's daughter, Mrs. Bernice Robinson Lee, also became a teacher. She was a teacher in the Chicago school system. Mrs. Lee has two daughters—one is a medical doctor and the other a dentist.

Gustavus A. Lumpkins and his wife, Catharine, went through slavery yet managed to educate their children. Their ancestors would be proud of the paths their descendants took to succeed.

BETTY DOGAN ROBERTS NICHOLAS

Parker, (no name given)—burial October 28, 1865, age eight months

In mid-October 1865, the weather was cold in the morning hours, and at night it was frosty. On October 28, 1865, an eight-month-old Parker child was buried on that cold frosty day.

A popular educator in Alexandria, Virginia, John F. Parker became the principal of Snowden School for boys during the Reconstruction era. He left a great legacy in Alexandria, and his descendants have kept his contribution in Alexandria alive.

Mrs. Betty Dogan Roberts Nicholas and her siblings are the great-grandchildren of William Martin Madison Parker, the brother of John F. Parker. William was a slave in Alexandria. His owner died in 1860. In his owner's will, he instructed that William would go to his sister, Mary, in Fairfax, Virginia, in the Mount Vernon area for five years, and then his sister should emancipate him. No provision was made to emancipate William's siblings and his mother in the owner's will. William did go to Mount Vernon area, but only for a short period of time. When the Civil War started, William returned to Alexandria with his future wife, Priscilla Smith. The granddaughter of Wes Ford of Gum Spring was a former slave of President George Washington. William married Priscilla Smith on August 10, 1862, in Alexandria. Three years later, William and Priscilla buried their eight-month-old child at the Freedmen's Cemetery.

After the death of Priscilla, William remarried, to Sarah Hooe on May 18, 1877. It is believed that Sarah was not a Negro. Because Sarah married a colored person, her race was listed as mulatto (mixed race). She was never in contact with anyone in her family from the time she married William.

Mary Ida Parker Dogan was the daughter of William and Sarah Parker. Mary's grandchildren and their families are the living descendants of the Parker child buried at the Freedmen's Cemetery. Mary had a son named William S. Dogan. William's nine children and their families are the living descendants of the Parker infant. They are John Leonard Dogan (deceased), Herbert Gray Dogan, Margo Dogan Farrar, Hope Dogan Kane, Betty Dogan Nicholas, Elaine Dogan Augustus, Fredrick Dogan, Thelma Dogan Lucas, and William Sanford Dogan Jr.

Mrs. Betty Dogan Roberts Nicholas is a retired government contract security officer. She attended Parker-Gray High School (partially named after her second great-uncle, John F. Parker) in Alexandria, Virginia. She is a

MAY 12, 1990

Betty Dogan Roberts Nicholas (*fourth from left*) and her children (1990). *Courtesy Betty Nicholas.*

member of St. Joseph's Catholic Church. Mrs. Betty organized and directed the church's youth choir and the John Carroll Chorus, and the chorus still exists. She is the mother of five sons and one daughter.

The Dogan-Parker family have been making progress through the generations. One of Betty's sons was accepted into Cortez Peters Business School at the age of eleven. He later became a police officer, retiring with twenty-eight years of service. Another son was the first African American to attend Pitt University on a tennis scholarship. He is now a professional tennis player, tennis teacher and a professional photographer.

Betty's siblings included John Leonard Dogan, who was a facilities manager and has one child and two grandchildren; Herbert Gray Dogan, who was a manager and has three children and six grandchildren; Margo Dogan Farrar, who was an administrative assistant and has five children and nine grandchildren; Hope Dogan Kane, who was an office manager and had two children; Chaplain Thelma Dogan Lucas, who has one child and three grandchildren; Elaine Dogan Augustus, who has no children; and Fredrick Dogan, who has five children.

Their paternal grandmother, Mary Ida Dogan, was a member of St. Joseph's Catholic Church in Alexandria. There is a memorial window in the

2014 Descendants at the Freedmen's Cemetery Dedication Ceremony. *Courtesy Tisara Photography.*

Thelma (Sugar) Dogan Lucas and William D. Euille (former mayor). *Courtesy Tisara Photography.*

body of the church with her name on it. The Dogan family used to attend St. Joseph's Catholic Church, but now Chaplain Thelma Dogan Lucas attends St. Joseph in Largo, Maryland. John Leonard Dogan was a member of St. Joseph's Catholic Church in Alexandria, and William Dogan Jr. attends Nativity Catholic Church in Washington, D.C.

The Dogan descendants within the Taylor family are the descendants of the Parker child who is buried in the Freedmen's Cemetery. The Taylors' connection will be discussed in the next narrative. For the Parker child, your Dogan family have done well throughout the generations.

Dorothy Napper Taylor and Yvette Taylor Lewis

Loomax, Arthur—buried September 13, 1864, age sixty
Loomax, Lucy—buried September 30, 1865, age sixty

On the morning of Emma Harris's burial, a cool breeze under the shaded trees helped lower the high temperature that day. The temperatures were around ninety degrees each day. Emma was buried during that breezy day on July 14, 1866, at the Freedmen's Cemetery.

The author was introduced to Mrs. Dorothy Knapper Taylor through her daughter-in-law, Mrs. Beatrice Cross Taylor. At the time of the interview with Mrs. Dorothy, she was ninety-four years old. She had a wealth of knowledge about Alexandria. She also had the rare opportunity of growing up with her great-grandmother Emily Washington, who was born a slave. Mrs. Taylor was born in 1914, and her great-grandmother died in 1928. Mrs. Dorothy shared with the author stories about her family. It appeared that Emily and some of her siblings were separated during slavery. It also appeared that some of her family

Dorothy Knapper Taylor (1914–2013). *Courtesy the Taylor family.*

First row, left to right: Dorothy Knapper Taylor, Emma Washington Thomas and Virginia Thomas Knapper. *Back row, left to right*: Dorothy Taylor's children. *Courtesy the Taylor family.*

members' given names and surnames were also changed during slavery. Mrs. Dorothy also shared family stories about other relatives who were sold during slavery.

Emily Lomax arrived in Alexandria with her sisters, Adeline Lomax and Eliza Loomis (Lomax). They came to Alexandria by joining a wagon full of people going north. The sisters were from Caroline, Virginia. Based on Mrs. Dorothy's recollection of her family history, it appeared that Emily, her siblings and parents arrived in Alexandria separately. Arthur Whittefield Lomax and Lucy Lomax (Susan Adams) died one year apart. They are buried at the Freedmen's Cemetery.

Harris, Emma—buried July 14, 1866, age eight months

Adeline was married to Thomas Harris. The Gladwin burial records stated that Adeline Harris buried her daughter, Emma Harris, at the Freedmen's Cemetery. Adeline and Thomas had several children after the death of Emma. Adeline died in 1938 at the age of eighty-four.

Martin, James—buried July 28, 1864, no age given

Emily's sister Eliza Lomax married George Martin on December 20, 1866. George was a shoemaker from Montgomery, Maryland, who lived in Alexandria during the Civil War. George had a brother named James Martin. James was buried at the Freedmen's Cemetery. Eliza and George had several children in Alexandria, Virginia.

Washington, Georgiana—buried July 31, 1864, age twenty-two
Washington, Helen—buried August 25, 1864, age thirty
Washington, Thomas—May 27, 1867, age twenty-two

A genealogy colleague, Selma Stewart, shared information with the author about a volunteer colony of Negroes who went from Fort Monroe in Hampton, Virginia, to Haiti in 1863. She has in her possession an article that listed the 450-plus individuals who were sent to Haiti. On that list was Emily Lomax's future husband, Lee Washington.

Lee Washington had volunteered to go to Haiti. The group of volunteers was promised housing, land and food. On their voyage from Fort Monroe, a smallpox epidemic broke out, killing many of them. Upon their arrival to Haiti, they found that it was the rainy season; the land did not yield the same types of crops they were used to in Virginia. Also, they were not given housing as promised. They had to fend for themselves. A report of their condition was sent to President Lincoln, and the president requested an investigation. Based on the investigation, President Lincoln ordered that the Negroes should return to the United States. The ship *Marcia C. Day* was sent to get them from Haiti. On the ship's return, it did not go to Fort Monroe; instead, the ship landed in Alexandria, Virginia, with the survivors numbering 368.

Whether Lee Washington knew Emily Lomax in Caroline, Virginia, no one knows, but Lee and Emily said when they got married on May 28, 1867, that they both came from Caroline, Virginia.

Although Lee came to Alexandria by way of Haiti, it appears that he had relatives who were already in Alexandria. Lee's parents were John and Caroline. John was mentioned in the 1865 Alexandria City and County African American Census. John and his wife buried their family members at the Freedmen's Cemetery.

One year after Lee arrived in Alexandria, he is found on the "Alexandria Real and Personal Property Tax" list of 1865. He paid twenty-five dollars in taxes on a house in Ward 2. Lee's occupation was laborer. By having family members in Alexandria, he was able to purchase property within a year after arriving in Alexandria. His property was located on Fairfax Street near Canal Basin, where his family lived until the twentieth century. Lee and Emily had four children: Jane, Adeline, Emma and John H. The children were named after their family members. Adeline and Emma were named after Emily's family. John was named after Lee's father, John. In April 1883, Lee Washington died at the age of forty-nine of "consumption." Prior to Emily's death, four generations of women lived in the same household, which included a great-granddaughter, Dorothy. They lived at 911 North Fairfax Street in 1928.

In 2013, Mrs. Dorothy Knapper Taylor was shy of her one hundredth birthday when she died on April 8, 2013.

For the Parker family discussed earlier, Mrs. Dorothy Knapper Taylor's husband, Charles Taylor, is the grandson of William Martin Madison Parker. Charles's mother, Blanche Parker, is William Parker's daughter. The Dogans and Taylors are kin, which makes them related to the Parker infant child buried at the Freedmen's Cemetery.

The Taylor family are a close-knit family. They have accomplished a lot since Lee Washington came to Alexandria. Lee and Emily's descendants from their great-granddaughter Dorothy Knapper Taylor owned their

Donald Taylor and Yvette Taylor Lewis. *Courtesy Tisara Photography.*

property, as well as provided for their families. Dorothy Knapper Taylor retired from the federal government with more than thirty years of service. She had four children. Her eldest son, Donald Taylor, served in the military. He retired from Fort Belvoir's military base. He has two daughters. Charlene Taylor Napper worked for seventeen years at the police department as a crossing guard, and then she worked for twelve years as an answering service operator for Alexandria. Mrs. Napper had three sons; only one son, Erich Dwayne Napper, is living. Her two deceased sons, Charles R. Napper and Leonard Lee Napper, were in the United States Air Force. Charles R. Napper retired as a master sergeant in the United States Air Force with the Strategic Air Command with more than twenty-three years of service. Charles A. Taylor is a retired U.S. Postal Service employee. He has three daughters. John L. Taylor was one of the early Metro train conductors. He retired as a bus driver. He has two daughters.

Many of Dorothy Knapper Taylor's grandchildren have obtained careers in federal and state governments and private companies. Donald Taylor's daughter Yvette Taylor Lewis retired from the Fairfax County Public School System as a sub school principal from Hayfield Secondary School with more than thirty-two years of service. Yvette holds a bachelor's degree in speech pathology/audiology from Norfolk State University, a certificate in learning disabilities from the University of Virginia, a master's degree in middle school curriculum and instruction and a certificate in administration and supervision from Virginia Tech University. She has three children.

Donna Taylor is the daughter of Charles A. Taylor. She retired from the Department of the Navy as a program analyst with more than thirty-three years of service. Her sister, Crystal Lorell Taylor Redmen, is the third daughter of Charles A. Taylor. She worked for the Department of Homeland Security, Federal Emergency Management Agency, as a program specialist, Human Resource Office. She retired after thirty-six years of service. She is also active in her church, Roberts Memorial United Methodist Church. Crystal is a trustee of the church and co-chair and secretary of the Bazaar and Decorating Committee and sings in the choir. She is a member of daughter of Israel Temple No. 138 of the IBPOE Elks Lodge No. 48 in Alexandria, Virginia.

Lee and Emily Washington and their family members at the Freedmen's Cemetery are proud that their descendants are a close-knit family and that the family have obtained the American dream.

Chapter 5

WE THANKED
THE PRESIDENT

They are your ancestors who arrived in Alexandria with the Union soldiers in September 1863. They clung to one another as they approached Alexandria, not knowing what the future holds. They had tears in their eyes as they took the rags from their sacks to wipe away their tears. They thanked the Lord and President Lincoln for giving them freedom. They also thanked the Lord and the president for all the ancestors who died for freedom and the children they lost. Some of those children died on their way to freedom. Now they are free—free like all of the ones who died for freedom.

When they arrived in Alexandria, they were assigned a place to stay at Sickle Barracks. The Freedmen's Bureau assigned them jobs. They had free time at night. They ate their evening meal and prayed to thank the Lord for their freedom, prayed for the ancestors who died in slavery and the ones who died on the journey to freedom, prayed that all of them would eat well in heaven and, above all, prayed for President Lincoln to win the war.

In the evening, they sat around the barracks, talked about meeting President Lincoln one day to thank him for their freedom. They pretended that they would dress in their finest clothes; the women would have their white gloves on as "proper women" would do. They would hold their heads high and say, "Mr. President Lincoln, we want to thank you for the stand you took against slavery, and if you ever in need of skilled workers, we will do the job." They laughed out loud, knowing they will not ask the president for a job, but they just wanted to thank him for their freedom.

Their dreams were shattered on April 14, 1865, when the president was shot. In the middle of the night, they heard people crying and guns going off. They thought someone was coming to take them back to their masters. They heard some said, "President Lincoln is dead!" The tears came pouring down their faces. They grabbed their children and held them tight. Somebody had killed the president, the president who freed the Negroes.

At dawn, they found out that the president died several hours after he was shot. He died on April 15. For the entire day, they heard people crying. They heard people talking about leaving and going north. They believed that their masters were coming for them. One group wanted to leave, and another wanted to stay. They prayed, and many decided to stay where they were. They did not know what was going to happen to them, but they believed that faith and prayers got them there, therefore it will protect them in the barracks.

For the next few days, the country was preparing for the burial of the president. The president's casket was put on a train and taken back to his hometown in Springfield, Illinois. They stood on a hill away from the crowd, and as the train slowly went down the tracks, they waved to the president's train and said, "Thank you, Mr. President for our freedom."

JAMES E. HENSON SR.

Seaton, Ephraim—burial September 26, 1866, age ninety

The first week of December 1868, the weather was pleasant in the morning and a little frosty at night. The night of Minor Skelton's death on December 7, 1868, the moon was bright and shiny. It had a reflection on the thin ice that covered the street.

Mr. James E. Henson, Esq., is well known in Alexandria, Virginia, and in Charles County, Maryland, where he has family ties. His maternal family's ancestor was Matthew Henson, the well-known North Pole explorer. His paternal side is connected to ancestors buried at the Freedmen's Cemetery.

His connection to the Cemetery begins with his father, Clarence McGuire. Mr. Henson's great-aunt, Alice V. McGuire, married John A. Seaton on March 18, 1877, in Washington,

Alice McGuire Seaton (1857–1939). *Courtesy James E. Henson Esq.*

D.C. Both of them were from Alexandria. In 1880, John and Alice Seaton lived at 131 St. Asaph Street in Alexandria. John's family members were freed African Americans prior to the Civil War; they were builders and politicians in Alexandria. John was born in 1837, and it is believed that Ephraim Seaton was John's grandfather. On September 26, 1866, Ephraim was buried at the Freedmen's Cemetery. Mr. Henson is indirectly related to Ephraim Seaton through his aunt, Alice, who married John Seaton. Mr. Henson is also related to the Coleman family.

Coleman, Joseph—burial June 27, 1865, no age given
Coleman, Mary Jane—burial June 24, 1864, age one year, nine months

Eliza McGuire (1830–1906). *Courtesy James E. Henson Esq.*

Mr. Henson's paternal grandparents were Reuben McGuire and Susie (Susan) Skelton. In 1920, they lived on South Royal Street. Susie's mother Nancy Coleman Skelton's parents buried Mary Jane in 1864 and Joseph in 1865 at the Freedmen's Cemetery. There were several Skeltons at the Freedmen's Cemetery who connected directly to Mr. Henson.

Skelton, Emily—burial July 9, 1864, age six
Skelton, Major—burial September 1, 1864, age six days
Skelton, Minor—burial December 7, 1868, age one year

Mr. Henson's grandmother Susie Skelton McGuire's parents were Thomas Skelton and Nancy Coleman. They were married on April 27, 1868. Thomas's parents were Major and Sarah. Nancy's parents were Minor and Maria. On July 9, 1864, Major and Sarah buried their six-year-old daughter, Emily, at the Freedmen's Cemetery. Unfortunately, they returned to the Freedmen's Cemetery in two months to bury their son, Major, who was six days old.

On December 7, 1868, Thomas and Nancy's firstborn child, Minor, died at the age of one year. Nancy was listed in the Gladwin burial records as the mother of Minor. They reported their address as Union Street near Wilkes Street tunnel. In 1874, Nancy faced another death when her husband, Thomas Skelton, died on November 12, 1874. They lived at Union near Gibbon Street.

James Ellis Henson Sr. was the only living child of his parents, Clarence McGuire and Catherine Henson. He was raised by his mother and cherished by his father, aunts and uncles. He spent a great deal of time with his

From left to right: James E. Henson Jr., Deardria Henson, Sharon Henson and James E. Henson, Esq. *Courtesy Tisara Photography.*

relatives, listening to their stories about their history. Mr. Henson grew up in the Catholic faith, attending St. Joseph's Catholic Church and St. Joseph's Catholic Elementary School. Although Mr. Henson was raised Catholic, his father's sisters were Baptist. Several of the McGuire's sisters were married by Pastor Samuel W. Madden at Alfred Street Baptist Church.

Mr. Henson spent his adult years raising his six children and building a solid career. He is a retired attorney with the Baltimore law firm of Singleton, Dashiell and Robinson. He was the first African American lawyer to serve as assistant county solicitor of Howard County in Maryland. James taught business law as an associate professor at Morgan State University and Howard Community College, Columbia, Maryland. Prior to his law career, Mr. Henson served in the United States Air Force, from which he retired as a master sergeant.

James E. Henson's six children continue to add to the family legacy. His first daughter, Deborah M. Henson, is a federal government employee; she has two children. His second daughter, Valerie S. Henson, has one child. His son James E. Henson Jr. is a businessman; he owns a copy and printing business and he has two children. His third daughter, Sharon A. Henson, is a federal government employee and has one child. His fourth daughter, Kayla

C. Henson, is a medical assistant with two children. And his fifth daughter, Nicole Henson Walker, is in the military and has two children.

Mr. Henson's ancestors without doubt will be proud of the myriad accomplishments he and his children have made.

FERDINAND T. DAY AND GWEN DAY FULLER

Baltimore and Lumpkins Families

There are many families throughout Alexandria, Virginia, who are indirectly related to the descendants in this book, and Mr. Ferdinand Day is one of them. His family migrated to Alexandria from Culpeper, Virginia, after 1870. The Alexandria Freedmen's Cemetery was officially open from 1864 to 1869. Mr. Day indirectly connects to two families at the Freedmen's Cemetery.

Mr. Ferdinand T. Day and his daughter, Gwen Day Fuller, are indirectly related to the Baltimore family from chapter 1 and the Lumpkins family from chapter 4. Mr. Day was named after his uncle, Ferdinand T. Day. His uncle's daughter, Evelyn M. Day, married Leon C. Baltimore Jr. on September 2, 1949. Leon Baltimore has descendants buried at the Freedmen's Cemetery.

Mr. Day's brother, Lawrence D. Day, married Helen Lumpkins Robinson on December 25, 1939. Mrs. Helen Lumpkins Day has ancestors buried at the Freedmen's Cemetery. Her grandparents Gustavus Lumpkins and Catharine Buckner buried their two-year-old child at the Freedmen's Cemetery.

Mr. Day made many contributions to the city of Alexandria. He was born on August 7, 1918. His parents were Robert A. Day and Victorine Smith. He was educated at Parker-Gray School up to the seventh grade in Alexandria. He completed his high school education in Washington, D.C., at Armstrong Technical High School. Later, he received his Bachelor of Arts degree from Miner Teachers College. After completing his education, he immediately went on to serve his community by becoming a community activist on issues related to education and housing. He became the first African American appointed to the Alexandria School Board and then as its chairman. During his tenure, he helped to integrate the school system. He served as vice-chairman of both the Northern Virginia and Virginia State Boards of Community Colleges. He worked with politicians to secure city government

Right: Ferdinand T. Day and Gwen Day Fuller. *Courtesy Tisara Photography.*

Below: *From left to right*: Henry B. Norton, Ferdinand T. Day and Elbert Norton Jr. *Courtesy Tisara Photography.*

funding to help with community projects in Alexandria. He was an advisor to community leaders, and he became a leader of the Boy Scouts. He also held a full-time job in the federal government while participating in many of the community activities. Mr. Day is a 2007 Alexandria Living Legend. Prior to his death, he was a member of St. Joseph's Catholic Church. On January 2, 2015, Mr. Ferdinand T. Day died.

Ms. Gwen Day Fuller is the only child of Ferdinand T. Day and Lucille Peatross. Gwen retired from the Newton, Massachusetts Public School System in 2006. She was educated in the Catholic school system (St. Joseph's Catholic Elementary School and St. Mary's Academy). She received her first degree from Hampton University in 1966 and her master's degree in education from Howard University in 1968. Just like her father, she is active in her community. She served as secretary of the Alexandria Library Board and is on the Cultural Arts Committee in Alexandria. She is chair of Concerned Citizens Network of Alexandria (CCNA), and she volunteer with the signature program (Reach and Rise for Excellence) at Hammond School. Gwen Day Fuller continues her fellowship with St. Joseph's Catholic Church, where she serves on the welcoming committee.

The city of Alexandria has benefited greatly from the community services of the Day family. They have set a high bar for their next generation. Gwen has two children and grandchildren.

GALE ARLENE BROOKS OGDEN

Alexander, Charlie—burial January 2, 1865, age seven
Alexander, Eliza—burial May 30, 1865, age twenty-two

On the last several days of 1864 through the New Year of 1865, heavy snow fell in Alexandria, Virginia. On January 2, 1865, children came out to play and slid down hilly sloops with their sleighs. But for seven-year-old Charlie Alexander, his funeral was on that day at the Freedmen's Cemetery.

Gale Arlene Brooks Ogden is an active member of Alfred Street Baptist Church. She is her family's historian. Her parents are Charles H. Brooks and Rebedell Hall Brooks. She connects to the Freedmen's Cemetery on her father's mother's side of the family through Eliza A. Whitmore Brooks. Eliza's grandparents were Charles T. Whitmore and Cassie P. Riddick Whitmore. Cassie's parents were Paul Riddick and Eliza Alexander Riddick.

From left to right: Necholus Ogden III, Gale Brooks Ogden, Necholus Ogden Jr. and Sydney N. Ogden. *Courtesy Tisara Photography.*

Paul and Eliza married on March 18, 1869. He was born in Hertford, North Carolina, and she was born in Loudoun, Virginia. Pastor Samuel W. Madden officiated the ceremony. Eliza had mentioned on her marriage license that her parents were John and Martha Alexander.

On January 2, 1865, seven-year-old Charlie Alexander was buried at the Freedmen's Cemetery. Charlie was Martha and John's son. After the Civil War, Martha Alexander worked at the L'Ouverture Hospital from 1865 to 1867. On May 30, 1865, twenty-two-year-old Eliza Alexander died at the L'Ouverture Hospital. She was a relative of Martha. It is believed that Martha's daughter, Eliza Alexander Riddick, was named after Eliza Alexander. Martha was making ten dollars per month as a cook at the L'Ouverture Hospital.

In 1870, Martha lived with her daughter and son-in-law, Paul and Eliza Reddick, at East Pitt Street. In 1880, John and Martha Alexander lived in the household with their daughter, son-in-law and five grandchildren. One of the grandchildren was Gale's great-grandmother Cassie P. Reddick. In 1900, Eliza Reddick was a widow, and she was staying at 123 North Pitt Street. She later moved to 819 Queen Street, where she passed away on January 28, 1928.

Gale Arlene Brooks Ogden and her brother, Dwight A. Brooks, can document their family in Alexandria, Virginia, back to the Civil War, and Gale's family membership with Alfred Street Baptist Church goes back to the war as well. Paul and Eliza Reddick's 1869 marriage was officiated by Pastor Samuel W. Madden, a well-known clergyman at Alfred Street Baptist Church. Today, Gale holds membership at Alfred Street Baptist Church and currently serves as the assistant church historian of the Alfred Street Baptist Church Historical Society.

Gale and her brother, Dwight, have other relatives who are buried at the Freedmen's Cemetery. Those relatives are in chapter 3 of Dena Banks's narrative.

Over the last one hundred years, John and Martha's descendants have held jobs as hostler and cook, federal and state government employees, school system administrator, hotel manager, property manager, lawyer, IT specialist, business owner and deacon, as well as served in the military. Their family members have done well in high school sports, swimming and football.

Many of these professions would not have been possible for John and Martha Alexander. They came to Alexandria to seek refuge from slavery and to have better life for their children and their descendants. Their ancestors would be proud of the progress that the descendants are making.

LILLIAN STANTON PATTERSON

Currier, Henry—burial July 29, 1866, age forty-five
Curry, Elizabeth—burial February 14, 1865, age twenty-five
Curry, Henry—burial September 29, 1865, age two
Curry, Hiram—burial April 25, 1866, age fifty

On Monday, it snowed heavily for some time in the morning. It was very cold, and the river was covered with ice. It was the coldest winter since 1855. One day later, the temperature was the same when Elizabeth Curry died on February 14, 1865.

Mrs. Lillian Stanton Patterson is a retired City of Alexandria employee. She was the curator at the Alexandria Black History Museum. She is also a fourth-generation Alexandrian. As a family and church historian, Lillian suspected a family connection to the Freedmen's Cemetery. During the research, the author confirmed that Mrs. Patterson's family were indeed

Left: Lillian Stanton Patterson; *Right*: Valeria B. Stanton Henderson (1931–2011). *Courtesy Tisara Photography.*

connected to the Freedmen's Cemetery. All the Curries who are buried at the Cemetery are her relatives.

Lillian's maternal grandparents were Charles and Lillian Gray. On September 22, 1898, Charles W. Gray and Lillian Curry married. Mrs. Patterson grew up in their household. Her grandmother Lillian Curry's parents were Randolph Curry and Annie Brannon. They were married on July 22, 1879, in Fairfax, Virginia. Randolph's parents were Henry and Lilla (Delilah). The forty-five-year-old Henry, who is buried at the Freedmen's Cemetery, was Randolph's father. Randolph's grandfather John Curry had two brothers Hiram and Henry. Hiram was buried at the Cemetery with two other relatives, Elizabeth and a two-year-old, Henry.

Mrs. Patterson's entire family lived in the household of her grandparents. Her grandfather Charles W. Gray owned a funeral home. In 1920, the family lived at 1021 Oronoco Street. On October 13, 1942, Charles Williams Gray died. He lived at 419 North Patrick Street. His wife, Lillian Curry Gray, lived for another seven years. She died on March 27, 1949. Her address at the time of her death was 519 North Patrick Street.

Mrs. Lillian Stanton Patterson is the daughter of the late Reverend Doctor N. Howard Stanton and Esther Gray. She is a 2012 Living Legend of Alexandria, Virginia, a community activist, a retired curator of the Alexandria Black History Museum, a former historian of Shiloh Baptist Church and a former teacher. She is a native Alexandrian and the oldest of seven children—N. Howard Jr., Charles H., Valeria B. Henderson, LeEtta N. Nowlin, Milton G.

and James W. She and her siblings attended Parker-Gray High School. Two siblings, Howard and LeEtta, attended Storer College in Harpers Ferry, West Virginia. Lillian and her sister Valeria graduated from Storer College. She graduated in the class of 1950 with a BA in social studies. Valeria graduated in the class of 1954 with a BA in English. Mrs. Patterson did advance courses in sociology at American University and early childhood development courses at the University of Virginia (Extension Department).

She is the widow of Edward Lloyd Patterson. She has two daughters, Marilyn Patterson and Valerie Patterson Connors. She has three grandchildren and one great-grandchild. Lillian continues to provide her expertise in areas where she is needed at the Alexandria Black History Museum and with her daughter Marilyn's business, Joyous Events, LLC.

Lillian Curry Gray's ancestors who are buried at the Freedmen's Cemetery are proud of the achievements that their descendants have made.

ZSUN-NEE (ZUNNY) KIMBALL MILLER MATEMA

Harrison, Elick—burial August 27, 1865, age thirteen
Harrison, infant—burial November 13, 1868, stillborn
Harrison, Joseph—burial January 27, 1864, age forty
Harrison, Sina Ann—burial January 27, 1864, age twenty-seven
Harrison, William—burial July 22, 1864, age one month

The weather was springlike on that winter day of January 27, 1864. The streets were crowded with pedestrians, and workers were repaving King Street. During that busy day, Joseph Harrison was buried.

ZSun-nee (Zunny) K. Miller Matema's family history is well known. Her ancestors are documented in the papers of President George Washington. Their early ancestor Caroline Branham (Branum) was a slave at Mount Vernon. Caroline's job at Mount Vernon was to fetch warming pans, light fires and candles, provide fresh jugs of water for washing and empty chambers pots. Also, she and the other house slaves were responsible for making the beds, washing clothes and linens, sweeping and scrubbing floors and dusting furniture. She was also a seamstress. On December 14, 1799, George Washington became ill. When he died later that evening, there were four slaves in the room—Caroline was one of them. She was married to Peter Hardiman, one of the slaves George Washington rented. They had

ZSunn-nee Matema with Derrick Ward, NBC4 reporter. *Courtesy Tisara Photography.*

From left to right: Bernice Robinson Lee, ZSun-nee Matema and Norma Jennings Turner. *Courtesy Tisara Photography.*

several children. After the death of Martha Washington in 1802, Caroline Branham, her husband and her children were given to George Washington Parke Custis.

Caroline Branham was born in 1772 and died in 1843. She was the personal maid of Martha Washington and the mother of Lucy Branham. Prior to the Civil War, Caroline's children and grandchildren were emancipated; her daughter, Lucy, is the direct ancestor of Zunny. Lucy was married to a man whose last name was Harrison. They had several children, and some of them appeared in the 1850 and 1860 censuses in Alexandria and Washington, D.C. Most of the children were registered as free people in Alexandria. The Harrisons who are buried at the Freedmen's Cemetery are Lucy's family. Lucy is Zunny's third great-grandmother, and Caroline is Zunny's fourth great-grandmother.

Zunny's family have made major contributions to society, especially Lucy's son Robert Robinson and his descendants. Emmett Robinson Miller was born on February 10, 1908, the son of Mary Virginia Robinson Miller, co-owner of a Washington, D.C.'s restaurant, M&N Seafood, and catering business. On July 14, 1995, Emmett died.

Magnus Lewis Robinson is the grandson of Lucy Harrison and the son of Robert H. Robinson, born on November 21, 1852. He was a journalist, editor, entrepreneur and founding president of the William McKinley Normal and Industrial School. There are several publications to his credit, including the *National Leader*, the *Virginia Pilot*, *Baltimore Sun* and many more. He held several political positions: he was the first African American secretary of Charlottesville, Virginia Congressional Convention in 1880; he represented Rockingham County in the Colored Convention; he was nominated magistrate of Alexandria, Virginia; he was grand master of the Magnus Robinson Masonic Lodge in Virginia; he was president of the Eighth Virginia District Convention of Colored Men at the Odd Fellows' Hall; and he was president of the Frederick Douglass Library Association, among other organizations and initiatives. On August 17, 1918, he died.

Robert Henry Robinson was the son of Lucy Branham. He was born on March 14, 1825. He was released from slavery by George Washington Parke Custis and became an apprentice at Robert's Bakery in Alexandria. He became a writer and orator and the first pastor ordained by Roberts Chapel Methodist Church in Alexandria at age twenty-one. He later became the pastor of nineteen churches between Petersburg, Virginia, and Parkersburg, West Virginia; he was grand master of both the Washington, D.C., Universal Lodge No. 1 and the Lodge in West Virginia; he was a

ZSun-nee Matema with the author, Char McCargo Bah. *Courtesy Tisara Photography.*

convener of the United Methodist Colored Convention, which established the United Methodist African American Churches; and he was treasurer of William McKinley Normal and Industrial School. On November 22, 1909, he died.

Zunny Miller Matema made her achievements as an entrepreneur, as founding president of AFRIASIA—An Intercultural Education Collective and as an owner of Annette's Dance Theater. She is an educator and world history instructor at Baltimore Polytechnic Institute; a writer, director and producer of children's programming at WRC-NBC, as well as radio talk shows *Talking Feather* and *Vital Signs*; and a contributing writer to *Master Washington's People*, a *National Geographic* publication. She is the author of *Elizabeth Keckley's Book of Good Measure*, an NBC/WRC winner of three cable awards and has served on civic boards, including Montgomery County Ethnic Affairs Committee and the Washington County Historical Advisory Board in Hagerstown, Maryland.

Caroline Branham and the ancestors at the Freedmen's Cemetery are truly blessed to know that Zunny added to the progress of their family's achievements.

Chapter 6

WE MARCHED
WITH THE YANKEES

I don't like talking about those slave days. Yes, Lord! We did not have a lot to be happy about. If our master let us go to church, we would be a little happy to get a break from the hot sun. But we couldn't even get happy in their church. We were told to be quiet and only to say "Amen." The real church came when we went to church in the bushes. We would get our old cooking pots, and when our Negro preacher started praising God, we would put our heads in the cooking pot so we could shout and cry so that God knows all of our sorrows and our pain. We only wanted God to know, not the master—the pots prevented the sound from traveling. Yes, we never really had any happiness until the Yankees arrived!

I just can't express the feeling of joy when those Yankees came to our master's plantation. We couldn't hold back our tears from all that suffering we have been through. Some of us were crying so hard that the Yankees said, "We have to go now." We dried those tears quickly and ran to get our belongings. Then the Yankees told us that we were free to come with them, that they would take us to a safer place. As we were walking behind the soldiers, we noticed our children holding their heads high and marching just like the Yankees. We were proud to see our children march like they were soldiers. We never gave our children anything that made them proud, but on that day, they had their freedom.

We watched how the soldiers marched, and soon we made a song to go with their steps. We marched as we sang our new song of freedom. As we approached other plantations, the slaves ran out and joined us in the march, all singing the new song together. We marched with the Yankees; we were marching with the Yankees to freedom.

The feeling of freedom was everywhere. Slaves ran into the road begging the Yankees to let them join us. Children with no parents running behind us were hollering, "Freedom!" Old women and old men were coming out of the bushes, slowly walking toward the Yankees shouting, "Freedom! Freedom!" Yes, we marched and sang our song of freedom with the Yankees.

Gloria Tancil Holmes and Herbert P. Tancil IV

Quander, Andrew—burial April 29, 1865, age two

On April 29, 1865, Andrew Quander died on a rainy week that helped the grass grow thick in the fields.

Gloria Tancil Holmes and her brother, Herbert P. Tancil IV, are descendants of the Quander family. The Quander family have a long documented history that goes back to slavery and their early emancipation from their slave owners. They can trace their roots back to Ghana in West Africa. There are several branches of the Quander family in Washington, D.C., Maryland and Virginia. All the Quanders are related to one another. Since 1926, the Quanders have celebrated their family at reunions. Gloria and Herbert descended from the Virginia Quanders. On April 29, 1865, Andrew Quander died. He is buried at the Freedmen's Cemetery. Andrew descended from the Quanders in Virginia.

Gloria and Herbert's parents are Herbert Pike Tancil III and Gladys Rebecca Quander. Gladys was born in Fairfax, Virginia, on ancestral property that has been in the family since the nineteenth century. Her parents were James Henry Quander and Alice Cordelia Smith. James H. Quander was born in 1882 in Fairfax, Virginia, also on ancestral property.

Seventieth Quander family reunion. *Courtesy Gloria Tancil Holmes.*

Left: Gladys Quander Tancil (1921–2002); *Right*: Herbert P. Tancil IV. *Courtesy Herbert P. Tancil IV.*

James's parents were Charles H. Quander and Amanda R. Quander. Charles was born in 1845; he owned his own property. His parents were Weston Quander and Maria Jackson. Charles H. Quander died on December 16, 1919.

The Quander family have made many achievements that make their free ancestors proud. In 2010, they had their eighty-fifth Quander family reunion. They continue to build on their proud legacy. At past reunions, Gladys shared and interpreted their history.

Gladys Quander Tancil was born in 1921. She was a historical interpreter for twenty-five years at Mount Vernon, the home of George Washington. She conducted slave tours, mastering the special skills in interpreting the lives of Mount Vernon slaves. Gladys was an advocate for the erection of the Mount Vernon Slave Memorial at President George Washington's plantation. She was one of the founders of the Black History Museum in Alexandria, Virginia. She participated in the Quander Family Reunion for most of her life. On November 5, 2001, Gladys Quander Tancil died. She left behind two children, Gloria Tancil Holmes and Herbert P. Tancil IV. She was a member of Alfred Street Baptist Church.

Gloria Alice Tancil Holmes was a retired Head Start education coordinator. She graduated from Parker-Gray High School in Alexandria in 1962, Virginia State University in 1966 and Jackson State University in Alabama in 1981. Gloria was married to Dr. Oakley Norman Holmes. They have one daughter and two grandchildren. Gloria was a member of Meade Memorial Episcopal Church in Alexandria. Prior to her death on August 14, 2016, she and her husband lived at their house on ancestral land that has been in the family since the 1880s.

Herbert (Herb) P. Tancil IV is the only son of Gladys Quander Tancil. Herb was the first Hartford Life Insurance Company's African American group sales manager in Detroit, Michigan, in 1985. He retired from the insurance company in 2004 after twenty-six years of service. In retirement, he continues his Hartford relationship as a contract benefits counselor representing the company during open enrollments, benefit fairs and meetings. He lives in Buckey, Arizona, with his wife, Marcia; sons, Herbert P. Tancil V and Chad L. Tancil, and their grandchildren, including grandson Herbert P. Tancil VI. He is carrying on the family name.

The Quander family have kept their family history alive for all their descendants. Their life started in Ghana, West Africa; they were sold and brought to the United States as slaves and were emancipated. The ancestors' Quander name survived from one continent to another.

Samuel (Sammie) Shanklin

Gray, Jennie—burial May 10, 1866, age twenty-seven
Shanklin, infant—burial August 19, 1867, stillborn

The weather was cold for the month of May. Apples, peaches and pears had been destroyed by that wintery weather. On May 10, 1866, Jennie Gray died.

Samuel (Sammie) Shanklin is the historian at Roberts Memorial United Methodist Church. Sammie's family are not related to the other Shanklins who are in this book. Before 1850, his family were free in Kings George County, Virginia. Shortly after 1860, Sammie's second great-grandfather David Shanklin Sr., who was born in 1815, migrated to Washington, D.C., with his wife, Anna, and their children. From Washington, D.C., David came to Alexandria, Virginia, with his family. While in Alexandria, his stillborn child was buried at the Freedmen's Cemetery.

Edgar D. Shanklin (1911–1992). *Courtesy Samuel (Sammy) Shanklin.*

When the war ended, some of the Shanklins went to King George County, Virginia. Some of them went to Washington, D.C., and others went to Alexandria. David's son, David Jr., went back to King George, Virginia, and David Sr. stayed in Washington, D.C. After a short time, David Jr. migrated to Alexandria. He married Mary Elizabeth Withers. The author did not find a marriage certificate, but the family Bible has their marriage recorded. David and Mary Elizabeth's son, David Shanklin Jr., purchased a house at 620 South Washington Street in Alexandria. Mary Elizabeth Withers Shanklin had a sister, Annie Withers. Annie married John Gray Sr. His grandfather John Edward buried his daughter, Jennie Gray, at the Freedmen's Cemetery.

Lightfoot (first name not recorded)—burial December 4, 1865, age thirty

Prior to 1900, Ella Gray was a single woman with three children when she married James Lightfoot. James was the son of Jefferson Lightfoot. Jefferson buried his sibling at the Freedmen's Cemetery. They lived at 724 Franklin Street. On April 4, 1951, Ella Lightfoot died. She was a widow at the time of her death. Ella's mother, Martha Gray, and John Edward Gray were siblings.

Left: Annie Withers (1848–1917). *Courtesy Samuel (Sammy) Shanklin.*

Right: John E. Gray (1913–1990). *Courtesy Elrich William Murphy Collection.*

On June 1, 1905, Samuel A. Shanklin Sr. was born to David Shanklin Jr. and Mary Elizabeth Withers in Alexandria. On November 15, 1944, Samuel A. Shanklin Sr. married Annie Senora Davis in Alexandria, Virginia. He lived at 620 South Washington Street, and she lived at 716 Wolfe Street. He was employed as a blacksmith for Mr. Al Valentine's shop on the corner of Wolfe and Columbus Street. Later, he obtained a job at the Arlington National Cemetery. He retired in 1969 after forty-two years of service. On September 5, 1988, Samuel Shanklin Sr. died.

Sammie Shanklin Jr. is the only child of Samuel Sr. and Annie Shanklin. He is a retired federal government employee with fifty years of service. His cousin John Gray is also a retired federal government employee. Both of them are members of Roberts Memorial United Methodist Church. Sammie still owns the property at 620 Washington Street that his grandfather purchased.

Samuel is an only child, but he has kept his family history alive for his cousins. His parents would be proud that he has passed down their family history.

SHIRLEY GILLIAM SANDERS STEELE

Lee, Major—burial June 13, 1866, age two and a half

On Monday, June 11, the temperatures kept rising. The City of Alexandria ordered the streets and alleys be disinfected to prevent cholera. But Thursday, June 13, 1866, Major Lee was buried during that hot weather.

Mrs. Shirley Gilliam Sanders Steel has known the author for more than fifty years. The author attended school with Mrs. Steel's daughter, Angela J. Sanders. Mrs. Steel's maternal side of the family have been in Alexandria since the Civil War. She and her sister, Mary Louise Lindsay Holt Cooper, are the daughters of Helena Wheeler Lindsay. Mrs. Shirley is very knowledgeable about her family's history because her grandmother Annie Lee Wheeler shared the family stories with her about Shirley's great-grandparents Senus (Senior) Lee and Melvina Craig Lee. After interviewing Mrs. Shirley, the genealogist verified all the information that was discussed, including information on her second great-grandparents Friday and Sarah Jane Lee. It was Mrs. Shirley's second great-grandparents who buried Major Lee at the Freedmen's Cemetery. The Gladwin burial records stated that Major's mother was Sarah Lee.

In 1870, Friday and Sarah Jane Lee lived in Ward 3 in Alexandria. They had four children in their household. Friday's occupation was a farm laborer. The city directory of 1876–77 stated that Friday lived on Henry Street near Princess Street. He had several children who appeared in the 1880 census: Senus, James, Lillie, Luther, Joseph and Daniel Lee. Mrs. Shirley's direct line comes from Senus Lee. In 1895, he married Melvina Craig. They lived at 318 North Henry Street. On June 7, 1896, Sarah

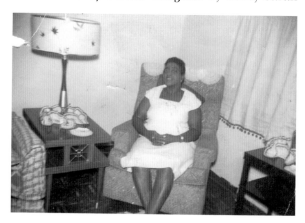

Helena Wheeler Lindsey (1922–1975). *Courtesy Shirley Sanders Steele.*

2014 attendees at the Freedmen's Cemetery Dedication Ceremony. *Courtesy Tisara Photography.*

Jane Lee died at the age of fifty-five from pneumonia. Her death notice stated her father's name as Edward Massy. Also she was born in Loudoun, Virginia, and she was a laundress.

On May 27, 1900, Friday Lee died at the age of sixty-five. He was buried at Bethel Cemetery in Alexandria, Virginia. His son Senus lived with his father-in-law, Daniel Craig (Craney). Daniel and Senus were day laborers. They lived at 312 North Henry Street. Job stability for Senus Lee improved in 1910 and 1920; he was employed as a laborer at the lumberyard. Prior to 1922, Senus's daughter, Annie Lee, married John Wheeler. Annie Lee Wheeler gave birth on November 8, 1922, to Helena Wheeler. Helena's father, John Wheeler, was in the military from January 15, 1904, to November 22, 1905. He was listed as a musician in the Twenty-Fourth Regiment United States Infantry. Helena was Mrs. Shirley Gilliam Sanders Steel and Mary Louisa Cooper's mother. They are direct descendants of Major Lee.

For more than one hundred years, Friday Lee and his descendants lived at only four different locations in Alexandria, including Sickle's Barracks during the Civil War, 300 block of North Henry Street and 400 North Patrick Street. On March 7, 1965, Annie Lee Wheeler died and her address was listed as 312½ North Henry Street.

First row sitting, left to right: DeCarlo Smith, Shirley Sanders Steele, Angela Sanders and Christine Sanders. *Standing, left to right*: Michael Lee, Tyrone Sanders and Kirk Sanders. *Courtesy Tisara Photography.*

The descendants of Friday and Sarah Jane Lee have been identified as Mary Louise Lindsay Cooper and her family, Shirley Gilliam Sanders Steel and her family, Michael Lee and his family and Karen Smith and her family. Mary Louise Cooper has four children: April Renee Holt, William Holt Jr., Diane Lennea Holt and Kim Holt.

Shirley Sanders Steel worked at the Hopkins Furniture Store in Alexandria for a number of years. In 1977, she obtained a clerical job at the telephone company. She retired with twenty-four years of service. She has three children, including Tyrone Sanders, who works with veterans and has five children and one grandchild; Angela Sanders, who has forty-two-plus years of service with the telephone company; and Kirk, who is retired from the telephone company with thirty years and seven months of service. He has one child and two grandchildren.

Mrs. Steel's grandparents, John and Annie Wheeler, were members of Third Baptist Church. She attended the same church until 1965. Today, she is a member of Community Praise Center Seventh-day Adventist Church in Alexandria, Virginia.

The Lees' ancestors are pleased to know that their descendants have maintained their family history.

Karen Hubbard Suggs and Faye Hubbard

Dudley, Clayborn—burial October 6, 1864, age nine
Dudley, Harry—burial July 25, 1865, age twenty-one days
Dudley, Isabella—burial August 16, 1864, age six
Dudley, Isabella—burial August 8, 1864, age one
Dudley, Kit—burial August 7, 1884, age three

The first week of October 1864 had tropical-like weather, with a cool breeze under the trees. But for nine-year-old Clayborn Dudley, that great day was a sad one for his family. On October 6, 1864, Clayborn died.

When the Freedmen's Cemetery project for the descendants began in 2008, Karen Hubbard Suggs, who lives in Alexandria, Virginia, thought that maybe her family connects to the Cemetery. She knew that her grandmother Sarah Dudley has the same surname as the other Dudleys buried at the Freedmen's Cemetery. Karen and the genealogist scheduled an interview. After the interview, the researcher analyzed pertinent documents that revealed that Karen's family were indeed connected to the Freedmen's Cemetery.

Karen Hubbard Suggs and her sister, Faye Hubbard, are direct descendants of Lewis (Louis) Dudley. They are the second great-grandchildren of Lewis Dudley Sr. and Betty Hudgins. Lewis. His large family migrated to Alexandria during the Civil War from Rappahannock County, Virginia. While in Alexandria, some of his grandchildren died and were buried at the Freedmen's Cemetery.

Prior to the Civil War, Lewis lived in Rappahannock County, Virginia. Lewis's wife, Bettie, and many of his adult children escaped from their masters and fled to Alexandria. Lewis was born between 1799 and 1804 in West Virginia. As a slave, he traveled from one county to the other with his master. During those travels, he had more than twenty children by several women. An article in one of the papers in Rappahannock County, Virginia, reported about the death of Lewis Dudley in Alexandria in 1890. The article stated that Lewis had run away from his master during the Civil War to Alexandria. The article also claimed that Lewis was a well-known slave in the community. Two of his children's marriage licenses were obtained. His son Lewis Jr. was born in Rappahannock County, Virginia, in 1852. His daughter Susan was born in Westmoreland County, Virginia, in 1856. In 1870, Lewis Dudley Sr. was listed as a grave digger at the age of sixty-six. In 1880, he was listed as a laborer, living at 172 Pitt Street. On February 10, 1883, Lewis's wife, Bettie Dudley, died. On March 16, 1890, Lewis Dudley Sr. died; his official age was eighty-four, but his actual age was ninety. At the end of his life, he had a respectable job, having become a Democratic Party campaign officer.

Karen Hubbard Suggs and Faye Hubbard's parents were Charlie Hubbard and Alice V. Brown. Alice was the granddaughter of Lewis Dudley Jr. and Martha Gaines. Martha died from childbirth around 1903, but her child survived. She was Karen and Faye's grandmother Sarah Virginia Dudley. On March 22, 1930, Lewis Dudley Jr. died. He is buried at St. Mary's Catholic Cemetery. He lived at 615 South Pitt Street.

From left to right: Alice Brown Hubbard, Charlie L. Hubbard and Marion D. Davis, February 14, 1953. *Courtesy Karen Hubbard Suggs.*

Lewis Sr. and Bettie Dudley's descendants have claimed a piece of the American dream. Sarah Dudley Massie worked as a bank employee and a volunteer for the American Cancer Society. She was a member of Roberts Chapel Methodist Episcopal Church. Theodore Dudley Sr. was employed with the Office of Personnel Management and Health and Human Services. He graduated from Howard University and served in the United States Navy. Augustine Brown was a tractor trailer driver and served in the United States Army. Alice B. Hubbard worked for the Alexandria Housing Authority and graduated from Cortez Peters Business School. She was also an insurance agent. Frances Dudley Gravitt was a government worker and the oldest member of Zion Baptist Church in Alexandria.

Karen Y. Hubbard Suggs is a native Alexandrian. She attended Alexandria City Public Schools, graduated from T.C. Williams High School in 1975 and then attended Northern Virginia Community College and George Mason University. Karen has worked for the air force and the Joint Chiefs of Staff at the Pentagon. She is currently employed by the Alexandria City Public School System, with thirty-two years of service. She is a member of Roberts Memorial United Methodist Church.

Old Lewis and his children took a chance to become free. He would be overjoyed to know that his descendants are now enjoying their lives because of the risks he took.

Chapter 7

NO MORE MASTER,
NO MORE MISTRESS

They walked or traveled by wagons to Alexandria. The old men, old women and young children traveled on wagons, and the rest of them walked to Alexandria, where they became free.

The master stood in the yard while the Yankees raided the plantation. They took farm animals, wagons, farm equipment, guns, sheets, whiskey and anything they could get their hands on. The master and his mistress stood there with stone faces in the yard while all their possessions were packed on four wagons. Their slaves stood there looking at the plantation that crumpled like the institution of slavery.

They were told that they were now free, that there were no more masters or mistresses. All their lives have been spent in slavery. They were finally free to make their own choices. They were at long last free to direct their own destiny—to have no one to make choices for them.

When they left their plantation, they looked back and saw old run-down plantation houses from one neighbor to the next. They knew that their lives will changed forever, but they were up for the changes that were ahead of them. They believed the worst was behind them, so they turned their heads and walked toward freedom. No more master and no more mistress.

KAREN AMBUSH THANDE

Thornton, Barbara—burial July 21, 1864, age ten

In July 1864, the city of Alexandria had a month of drought. Very little rain came in the last several weeks, so the city was covered by dust. The local markets suffered from lack of water for their produce. On July 21, 1864, when the weather was extremely hot, ten-year-old Barbara Thornton was buried.

The genealogist knew Karen Ambush Thande through the Alexandria Black History Museum. Karen and her siblings are the second great-nieces of Harriet Welford Thornton. On March 12, 1891, Harriet married John T. Thornton. She listed her parents as Richard and Mary Etta Welford. He listed his parents as John and Lucinda Thornton. The bride and groom were both born in Alexandria, Virginia. They were married at the Alfred Street Baptist Church, and Pastor Samuel W. Madden officiated the ceremony. John was a plasterer, and Harriet was a teacher. John, his parents and siblings were free people prior to the Civil War. They had several children. Their daughter Barbara died and was buried at the Freedmen's Cemetery.

Barbara's parents registered as freed people in Alexandria. John Thornton registered as a freed person on July 31, 1847. His physical description was listed as follows: "A bright mulatto who was 22-years old, 5 feet, 10¾ inches

Top, from left to right: Grace Virginia Woods, Mary Ellen Woods and Ruth Etta Woods. *Bottom, left to right*: Peter Charles and Virginia Etta Welford Woods. *Courtesy Karen Ambush Thande.*

tall, with a scar on his right elbow. He was born free." John's wife, Lucinda Cole, registered on February 6, 1855, and was described thus: "A very bright mulatto, about 16 years old, 5 feet, 4 inches tall, with a small scar in her left eyebrow…was born free." Unlike John T. Thornton's family, Harriet Welford Thornton's family were enslaved prior to the Civil War.

In 1870, John Sr. and his family lived at 187 Fayette Street. John T. Thornton died on April 24, 1892. His father, John Thornton, died at the age of sixty-eight on December 11, 1888. Harriet continued her career as a teacher at Parker-Gray School until she retired. She was one of the original teachers at Parker-Gray when the school opened its doors in 1920. Prior to 1920, Harriet was a teacher at Hallowell School for Girls. After she retired, she moved to Kansas City closer to her son, John T. Thornton Jr. Her son died on January 11, 1959. He graduated from Hampton Institute, majored in building architecture and taught at Storer College. In 2009, his daughter, Evangeline Ophelia Thornton Myles, was ninety-two years old.

Karen Ambush Thande and her siblings are the nieces and nephews of Harriet Welford Thornton. Karen's mother, Shigo Gladys Sato Ambush, is the great-niece of Harriet Welford Thornton. In Harriet's lifetime, she

From left to right: Sean Denniston, Karen Ambush Thande and Chandraleela Harrington.
Courtesy Tisara Photography.

probably kept in touch with her niece, Grace Virginia Woods Sato, and her sister, Virginia Etta Welford Woods. This is the family to whom Harriet had close family ties, especially when she lost her husband early in their marriage. Harriet's family are from many cultures: one Japanese, one Bajan and one American Indian (Wampanoag). The family are made up of three branches of the Sato/Marshal/Henry families.

Karen Ambush Thande is a retired Boston Public Schools educator. Her siblings include June Elizabeth Ambush, who is a retired Boston Public Schools educator; Kathy Grace Ambush Smith, who is a public relations consultant and fundraiser; Benjamin Sato Ambush, who is a professional stage and theater director and educator; and Stephen Bruce Ambush, who is an ordained minister and musician.

The ancestors of John T. Thornton have a special connection with the Ambash family. Their ancestors are proud of their achievements.

ADRIENNE TERRELL WASHINGTON AND CALVIN TERRELL

Shorts, John Henry—burial September 1, 1864, age one year
Shorts, Shadrah—burial June 21, 1864, age one year, three months

All month long, the weather was above eighty-five degrees, but one night, a fine shower cooled the temperature just in time for the burial of Shadrah Shorts on June 21, 1864.

Adrienne Terrell Washington is well known in the area called Fort Ward (Seminary) in Alexandria, Virginia. She is president of the Fort Ward and Seminary African American Descendants Society (the Fort Ward area is known today as part of Alexandria). Harriet Stuart McKnight Shorts is Adrienne's maternal second great-grandmother. Harriet's second husband was Burr Shorts. The two children buried at the Freedmen's Cemetery were Burr Short's children by his first wife. Harriet's first husband was Willis McKnight, who died around 1865. Harriet and her McKnight's children migrated from Fauquier, Virginia, to Fairfax, Virginia. Harriet and Burr lived together in the 1870 census. They married on July 6, 1882, but Burr died in 1898. He left all his property to his wife, Harriet. On July 18, 1917, Harriet died at the age of ninety-five. Her property was left to her McKnight children and her daughter, Clara Shorts Adams.

The Shorts-McKnight extended family were one of the founding families of the post–Civil War African American community at Fort Ward, known as "The Fort." Harriet was one of the founders of Oakland Baptist Church. Adrienne also connects to the Terrells who were buried at the Freedmen's Cemetery.

Terrill, Rachel—burial November 13, 1867, age thirty
Tewell, Rosina—burial April 4, 1864, age seventeen
Tirrell, Mary—burial June 1, 1865, age fifty
Torell, Moses—burial March 16, 1865, age twenty

Adrienne's mother is Gwendolyn (Gwen) Wihelmenia Terrell Johnson. Gwen's Terrell family have been in Alexandria since the Civil War, and they lived in the Fairfax, Virginia, area near Fort Ward. Jacob Terrell was born in 1790; he arrived in Alexandria with his wife, sons and grandchildren. His sons were Philip Terrell, born in 1818, and Joseph Terrell, born in 1823. Based on the research, Jacob's wife was Mary Terrell, the fifty-year-old who was buried at the Cemetery. Rachel Terrill, who was buried at the Freedmen's Cemetery, was Philip Terrell's wife. The others who are at the Freedmen's Cemetery are Jacob's children. Jacob and his two grandchildren lived in the same household in Alexandria, Virginia, in 1870. Those grandchildren were Jacob Terrell and Toliver Terrell. On their marriage licenses, they both mentioned that their parents were Jacob and Fannie Terrell. Jacob, who was born in 1790, had a son also named Jacob, who probably died before the 1870 census. Jacob Sr. died after 1870; his grandson Jacob married and moved to Fairfax, Virginia, near his relatives.

Gwendolyn's parents were Jacob Terrell and Beatrice Nash. Her grandparents were John William Terrell and Burney McKnight. Her great-grandparents were Joseph Terrell and Amanda Terrell. Joseph's brothers are Philip and Jacob. Their father, Jacob, migrated to Alexandria with Philip, Joseph, their wives and children during the Civil War. Their descendants have multiplied many times. Adrienne and her uncle Calvin Terrell Sr. are two of the many descendants of the Terrell family.

The Terrells are members of Oakland Baptist Church in Alexandria. Adrienne is a member of two churches; her maternal side attend Oakland Baptist Church, and her paternal side attend Meade Memorial Episcopal Church.

They have made accomplishments in many fields. Reverend Alphonso Terrell is a retired Metropolitan Police Department detective and now

2014 dedication of Freedmen's Cemetery with descendants. *Courtesy Tisara Photography.*

Calvin Terrell and Frances Colbert Terrell. *Courtesy the author.*

a minister, primarily at Oakland Baptist Church. Nechelle Terrell, his daughter, was commended for coordinating the Alexandria City Health Department's HIV/AIDS programs. Keith and Dwayne Terrell were members of the famous 1970s "Remember the Titans" football team at T.C. Williams High School. Jarreau Williams was an actor/singer in numerous plays, including those at the National Theatre. Lois Terrell Torney was the first female president of the Virginia chapter of the International Ushers Association. James Terrell was commended for more than forty years of service as "Dr. J.T." in the Alexandria Hospital room. Jacob E. Terrell "of Seminary" was commended for his military service in World War I, as reported in the *Alexandria Gazette*, and he was on the Oakland Baptist Church Deacon Board. Beatrice Nash Terrell, "Miz Bea," was a teacher at Seminary (Rosenwald) School, was an Oakland Baptist Church clerk for thirty-eight years, a first black poll worker for the City of Alexandria and a representative member of the Women's Ecumenical organization in Alexandria.

Adrienne Terrell Washington is the daughter of Gwendolyn Terrell Johnson and Earl Anthony Randall. She has two children, Mario Edwin Washington and Misti Eileen Washington. Her siblings are Angela Terrell Shivers, Darlene Randall, Donna Randall and Jay Allan Johnson. Adrienne is an award-winning Washington, D.C., journalist, television, radio commentator and college professor. Her columns and editorials for the *Washington Times* and the *Afro-American* focus on public policy issues, particularly social and economic injustices involving women, children and minorities. She received her master's degree in writing from Johns Hopkins University in May 2008. Since 2001, she has taught at the Catholic University of America and Northern Virginia Community College.

PAULA HASKINS WILLIAMS

Haskins, Ann—burial November 20, 1865, age two
Haskins, John H.—burial July 18, 1866, age two months

On November 20, 1865, two-year-old Ann Haskins was buried at the Freedmen's Cemetery during a northeast snowstorm. Because the ground was still warm and the weather was not extremely cold, the snow melted as soon as it fell.

The genealogist has known the Haskins family for more than forty years. They grew up in the same neighborhood and attended the same schools. Paula Haskins Williams was her family historian. Unfortunately, Paula died seven months after she was interviewed for the Freedmen's Cemetery project. On September 1, 2008, the author interviewed Paula about her family's connection to the Freedmen's Cemetery. She knew a lot and was excited to share her family's history. She was close to her father and her grandmother Virginia Holmes Haskins. They shared a great deal of information with her. Her father told her that they had relatives buried at the Freedmen's Cemetery.

The genealogist researched the family information that Paula had provided and was able to add to her family's history. Her third great-grandfather Charles George Haskins was born around 1833 and his wife, Mary Jane Haskins, around 1838. They came to Alexandria, Virginia, during the Civil War from Petersburg, Virginia. Three of their oldest children were born in Petersburg, and the rest of their children were born in Alexandria. Their two children, Ann Haskins and John H. Haskins, buried at the Freedmen's Cemetery, were born in Alexandria.

In 1870, Charles George, who preferred using the name Charles, lived in Alexandria in Ward 3 with Mary Jane and children Christina and Ada. He was a laborer. The city directory of Alexandria 1876–77 indicated that Charles Haskins was a driver. He lived on Pitt near Oronoco Street. At the end of the nineteenth century, Charles added more children to the household: Christina, Ada, Charles and John. John was listed as the son of Charles, and additional research revealed that the son, John, was the grandson of Charles and Mary. John was the son of Christena (Tenie). He was probably named after his deceased uncle, John H. Haskins, who was buried at the Freedmen's Cemetery. In 1895, the Alexandria city directory listed the family with two different addresses: Charles M. Haskins, believed to be the son of Charles and Mary, lived at 515 North Pitt Street, and Charles Haskins Sr. lived at 624 South Pitt.

On September 27, 1900, John Haskins married Ella Miller in Alexandria. They were Paula's great-grandparents. Mary and Charles died within four years of each other. Mary Jane Haskins died on November 10, 1901, from consumption; she was listed as seventy years old on her death notice, but she was actually sixty-three. On October 17, 1905, Charles Haskins died supposedly at the age of sixty-two from indigestion, but he was actually seventy-two.

John and Ella Miller Haskins had a son named Andrew J. Haskins. On March 3, 1923, Andrew J. Haskins married Virginia Holmes. They were the grandparents of Paula. She had fond memories of her grandmother. John lived at the family home at 515 North Pitt Street, and his wife Virginia's family lived at 623 North Pitt Street. Andrew and Virginia's son, James Edward Haskins, married Corrinne Johnson. They were married in Washington, D.C. James and Corrinne are Paula's parents. Corrinne Johnson Haskins is the great-granddaughter of Wallace Wanzer. She and her children are related to the Wanzers from chapter 4.

Paula comes from a large family of eight siblings: Peggy Emerson, James E. Haskins Jr. (deceased), Constance Ross (deceased), Shelia Rucker, Jeffrey Haskins, Carol Daniels, Deborah Haskins and Roland Andrew Haskins (deceased). They are members of the Oakland Baptist Church. Prior to James marrying Corrinne, he was a member of Ebenezer Baptist Church in Alexandria, Virginia.

Paula Regina Haskins Williams was married to Theodore Williams Jr., and she had one son, Quentin Williams, who preceded her in death. She worked for the City of Alexandria as a personnel analyst. Some of her siblings worked for the federal government and private industry.

Paula enjoyed reminiscing about her father and grandmother. Her ancestors would be pleased to know that she passed on the family history.

ANDREW JOHNSON AND JAMES HENRY LIGHTFOOT IV

Hughes, Winnie—burial March 20, 1867, age seventy
Lightfoot, Mary—burial July 17, 1868, age four
---, infant—burial July 3, 1866, age two weeks

In March 1867, an equinoctial storm hit the eastern area of the United States, bringing northeast winds, sleet and rain for several days, including the day Winnie was buried. Fisheries and all farming operations came to a halt. Winnie Hughes's family had a difficult time in burying her on March 20, 1867, at the Freedmen's Cemetery.

The first descendants found connected to the Freedmen's Cemetery were the Lightfoot family. In 2008, Amy Bertsch located the descendants of Matilda, Andrew Johnson, Antoinette Lightfoot and James Henry Lightfoot IV. In the Gladwin burial records, a Matilda Lightfoot was the one who buried her grandmother Winnie Hughes in 1867. Also, there were two additional entries of burials that listed Matilda Lightfoot. She was listed as the mother of two-year-old Lightfoot, buried on July 3, 1866, and four-month-old Mary Lightfoot, buried on July 17, 1868.

Since Matilda had survived her grandmother and her two children, Amy researched Matilda Lightfoot through the censuses, vital statistics, city directories and military records. What she found was that Matilda was married to Larkin Lightfoot, and they appeared in the 1870 and 1880 censuses. Larkin was a railroad worker, and the family members were listed as mulattos. Matilda died on April 16, 1894, at age fifty-one. She was buried at Bethel Cemetery in Alexandria.

Amy continued to research Matilda's surviving children, James H., Susan and Phoebe. In 1900, the three children lived together in the 200 block of South West Street. Matilda's son, James, was a plasterer. He married a widow on December 22, 1897. In the 1910 census, James Lightfoot and his eight-year-old son, James Lightfoot Jr., lived in the 200 block of South West Street. The 1920 census showed that James Lightfoot Sr. and his wife, Carrie, purchased their home at 228 South West Street. Father and son's occupations were listed as plasterers.

On February 23, 1924, James Lightfoot Sr. died. Carrie died on September 15, 1937. Their only surviving child was James H. Lightfoot Jr., who married Frances Elizabeth Harris. They had two children, Esther Virginia Lightfoot and James Henry III. On February 27, 1946, James Lightfoot Jr. died.

The focus now was on James Henry "Jim" Lightfoot III, who was born on January 16, 1925. James met Williease Craft in Washington, D.C., prior to going into the military. Later, she migrated to North Carolina, where she had their son, James Lightfoot Craft, in 1943. She allowed her son to be adopted by Alma Johnson. Alma changed the name of Williease's son to Andrew Johnson.

Jim Lightfoot III served in the military in the early 1940s. While he was in the service, he met Willie May Charles. They married and lived in Alexandria at 228 South West Street for several years. They had two children, Antoinette Lightfoot and James Henry Lightfoot IV. The family later moved to Woods Place in the Seminary community. Jim died in 1974 not knowing he had another child.

Today, the descendants of Larkin and Matilda Lightfoot are Andrew Johnson, Antoinette Lightfoot, James Henry Lightfoot IV and their children. Andrew is the oldest child of James "Jim" Henry Lightfoot III. He and his wife, Rosa Best Johnson, live in Atlanta, Georgia. He was born in Greensboro, North Carolina. He has two children, Andrew Johnson III, Karen Johnson Canion; five grandchildren; and four great-grandchildren. His adopted mother was Alma Johnson.

Antoinette Lightfoot Jones and her brother James Henry Lightfoot IV are native Alexandrians. Both attended St. Joseph's Catholic School, and

Lightfoot family. *Last row, second from the left*: Andrew Johnson and family. *First row, second from the left*: Antoinette Lightfoot. *Last row, right*: James Lightfoot and family. *Courtesy Tisara Photography.*

they are members of St. Joseph's Catholic Church. Antoinette has four children: Dori, Kimberly, Katrina and Rochael. James H. Lightfoot IV is the second son of James Henry "Jim" Lightfoot. He and his wife, Jeanette Rice Lightfoot, have two children, Jennifer and Matthew.

After the Civil War, Matilda buried three family members, her grandmother and her two children. She endured the pain of her loss and continued building a better future for her generation. She would be proud to know that her descendants have kept the Lightfoot family history alive.

Irene Gaskins Macklin

Tibbs, Aleck—burial June 15, 1868, age thirteen
Tibbs, Caroline—burial November 28, 1865, age ten
Tibbs, James—burial April 29, 1867, age seventeen
Tibbs, Mary—burial November 16, 1865, age seven

Hot weather oppressed Alexandria for the last week of June 10, 1868, with temperatures running in the nineties. Under the shades, the temperature was a little cool, around eighty-five degrees on June 15, 1868, when Aleck was buried.

The meeting between Mrs. Irene Joyce Gaskins Macklin and the author was a referral by another descendant. After their meeting, the author researched Irene's family and was able to connect her maternal side to the Freedmen's Cemetery. Irene's third great-grandparents buried four of their children at the Cemetery.

Armistead and Matilda Tibbs were in Alexandria, Virginia, during the Civil War. They had seven children. Four of their children were buried at the Freedmen's Cemetery. The surviving children were Wesley, Frederick and Sarah Tibbs. Armistead was recorded as a laborer in the 1873 Alexandria City Directory. He lived at 105 South Royal Street. His son Wesley Tibbs was a baker and lived at 100 North St. Asaph Street. Wesley is Irene's second great-grandfather.

Mrs. Macklin's grandmother was Ruth Tibbs Graham. She had a daughter, Johnnie Mae Graham, who married Alfred Gaskins on August 5, 1939, in Alexandria. Reverend A.W. Adkins officiated the ceremony. He was a well-known clergyman at Alfred Street Baptist Church. Based on their marriage certificate, Johnnie was born in Pennsylvania. Her parents were working in Pennsylvania when she was born. At the time of their marriage, Johnnie lived

Irene Gaskins Macklin (1941–2015). *Courtesy the author.*

at the rear of 331 North Henry Street. Alfred J. Gaskins lived at 812 Queen Street. Mrs. Macklin was named after her father's mother, Irene Gaskins. On September 24, 1948, Alfred and Johnnie Mae Gaskins divorced. Johnnie Mae remarried a Francis E. Knapper, who was a World War II veteran. On January 27, 1990, Francis died. He was buried at Quantico National Cemetery. Johnnie Mae Knapper died on May 5, 2003, and she was also buried at Quantico National Cemetery.

On September 6, 2015, Mrs. Irene Joyce Gaskins Macklin died. She was married to the late Herman Macklin Sr. Irene's children are Richard Gaskins, Lisa Gaskins (deceased) and Herman Macklin Jr. Also at the time of her death, she had four grandchildren and six great-grandchildren. Her brother, Donald Green, preceded her in death on October 27, 2013. She was a member of the Third Baptist Church in Alexandria.

When the genealogist told Irene that she had ancestors at the Freedmen Cemetery, she cried. Irene and her brother, Herman Jr., are now rejoicing with their ancestors at the Freedmen Cemetery.

Chapter 8

ALEXANDRIA CONTRABANDS AND FREEDMEN'S CEMETERY DEDICATION CEREMONY

For more than a century, the African Americans of Alexandria, Virginia, felt neglected. Their neighborhoods have gone through many urban renewal projects, leaving them with fewer affordable places to live. Throughout Alexandria's history, there has been a sizeable minority population. But over the last century, the landmarks that showcased the history of the city's minority group have been destroyed and replaced by residential or commercial buildings. The African Americans of Alexandria felt that their history has not been part of the history of Alexandria until the Freedmen's Cemetery was rediscovered.

The Freedmen's Cemetery project brought the African Americans and the city together like no other time in their history since the Civil War. Many African Americans did not believe that the city would honor their ancestors and their descendants. The city also wasn't sure that the descendants would come to the events that were planned.

Lance Mallamo, director of the Office of Historic Alexandria, spearheaded the Freedmen Descendant's Planning Committee. That committee consisted of Lance Mallamo, Audrey P. Davis, Francine Bromberg, Ruth Reeder, Cheryl Lawrence, Cheryl Anne Colton, Shelia Whiting, Andrea Blackford, Katy Cannady, Pat Miller, Carla McGinnis, Lillian and Marilyn Patterson and Char McCargo Bah. For more than a year, the group met weekly to plan the dedication ceremonies. The committee finalized two ceremonies in 2014: "Alexandria Contrabands and Freedmen Cemetery Memorial:

J. Lance Mallamo (retired director, Office of Historic Alexandria) talking to the Taylor family. *Courtesy Tisara Photography.*

From left to right: Francine Bromberg, former city archaeologist, and Audrey P. Davis, director of Alexandria Black History Museum. *Courtesy Tisara Photography.*

2014 Kick-Off," scheduled for March 4–6, and "The Journey to Be Free," scheduled for September 3–7.

No one in the city knew how many descendants would attend the ceremonies, but the March event gave an indication that the descendants were eager to honor their ancestors. A few days before the event, it snowed. The committee was not sure how many people would show up in such icy weather conditions. The main event was located at the Lee Recreation Center auditorium in Alexandria, Virginia, and featured a performance by the All-Souls Jubilee Singers from Howard University and a guest speaker, historian C.R. Gibbs. The descendants packed the auditorium with no seats left. Many of them came from out of the area, as far away as California.

The second event was scheduled in September, with many activities held throughout the city for the descendants. All the descendants were told to check in at the Alexandria Black History Museum. The descendants became very emotional, showing tears of joy and disbelief that the city was honoring them and their ancestors. The weeklong events included a candlelit cemetery ceremony, visits to the city's museums, lectures on the Civil War, neighborhood walking tours, a descendants' banquet, a dedication

Vice-Mayor Allison Silberberg (currently mayor of Alexandria). *Courtesy Tisara Photography.*

From left to right: Louise Massoud, William D. Euille (former mayor), Lillie Finklea and Dr. Pamela J. Cressey (retired former city archaeologist). *Courtesy Tisara Photography.*

ceremony of the Freedmen's Cemetery and the descendants' attendance at their ancestral church.

The highlight of the weeklong schedule was the banquet and the dedication ceremony. The Office of Historic Alexandria decorated the Charles Houston Recreation Center auditorium using pictures from Civil War era. There were recognitions of the people who made the event successful and political speakers, but one of the highlights of the banquet was a special gift to the descendants: the "Spoken Words" narrated for the descendants with their ancestors in mind. For that moment, they felt like their ancestors were in the room participating in the celebration with them. Each descendant present was given "a message" from his or her ancestor. Tears and joy filled the room during that special moment.

The dedication of the Freedmen's Cemetery was an emotional experience. Church bells rang to honor the ancestors at the Freedmen's Cemetery. A choir also rang bells at the dedication ceremony. Mayor William D. Euille; members of the city council; Congressman Moran; and Lance Mallamo, a poet and historian, spoke to the descendants. Representatives of the Masons—Worshipful Prince Hall, 31st District of Virginia, participated in the ceremonies. Civil War songs were sung by Andrea Jones Blackford's group, Washington Revels Jubilee Voices. The dedication ceremony ended

Members of Thirty-First Masonic District of Virginia–Prince Hall Masons. *Courtesy Tisara Photography.*

2014 Freedmen's Cemetery Descendants' Banquet attendees. *Courtesy Tisara Photography.*

with the descendants walking to the cemetery with a rose to be placed at the base of the statue there.

Every news media outlet in Washington, D.C., Northern Virginia and Maryland reported the Freedmen's Cemetery dedication ceremony. All the major television stations ran the news as well. Descendants were interviewed about their experience, and the city officials and political appointees of Alexandria were able to stand and say, "A job well done."

Close to one thousand people attended different events during the five-day celebrations. All descendants who participated in this journey left the events with a positive feeling about their ancestral home, knowing that Alexandria took the time to honor their ancestors respectfully. That helped past wounds to heal.

Epilogue

"CALL OUR NAME"

We lie here in these grounds waiting to hear our names, yet we've not heard from you, our descendants. We are waiting to hear from you. We have been here for more than 150 years. We died so that you'll be free. We would like to hear your voices and see your faces. We would like to learn about your lives and what you've become. We do not want to be forgotten like unattended grass on an abandoned piece of land. We do not want to wither away with the passing of time, only to be thought of when another one of us is rediscovered. We want to hear our descendants' voices. We have a lot of history that you can learn from.

You can learn who we are, learn about our pain, our strength, our endurance, about our forgiveness of mankind and about our prayers. Yes, we prayed a lot for this day to come so that you will taste the sweet water of freedom. We prayed that when your time comes for the next world, we will be there to receive you with open arms, holding you and crying with joy that you have now joined us. Our spirit and yours will rejoice that, at long last, we're now inseparable. Yes, for every descendant who passes through the cycle of life, we rejoice that this person has found their family again.

Do not forget about us, because we have never forgotten about you. Learn what we know. You will be enriched and enlightened by the struggles of our people. Teach your children about us and teach them about our history. There were many mistakes made, but one always learns a lesson from mistakes. So learn about your history and learn about us. We are waiting to hear our names called by you, the living.

For our descendants, step up to the plate and tell our story. This is not just our story, but a story that all humanity should learn about. We are waiting!

EPILOGUE

T here are more than 1,700 graves at the Freedmen's Cemetery, and only 171 deceased individuals have been connected to their descendants. This book covers the stories of 130 individuals whose descendants have been found. The remaining 41 individuals' stories will be told one day by their descendants. For the other 1,500 deceased individuals who are buried at the Freedmen's Cemetery, we are still searching.

The names of the forty-one deceased individuals whose descendants were found, though their stories are not covered in this book, include:

Ashby, Lucy—buried February 28, 1866, age two months
Beckham, William—burial January 28, 1867, age twenty-six months
Bolden, Alfred—buried April 13, 1864, age twenty-one
Bolden, Cornelius—buried May 11, 1866, age nineteen
Butler, Mary Jane—buried March 14, 1866, age twenty-five
Carroll, Mary E—buried July 9, 1855, age seven months
Dickenson, Harriett—buried August 12, 1863, age one year and six months
Dickenson, Malinda—buried April 6, 1866, age sixty
Fairfax, Kitty—buried November 6, 1864, no age given
Fairfax, Melinda—buried September 25, 1864, age twenty-seven
Fairfax, Neil—buried December 11, 1864, age four years and seven months
Fortune, James—buried February 21, 1865, age twenty-five
Gannt, Louisa—buried August 18, 1864, age six
Gannt, Rachel—buried July 13, 1864, age two months and ten days
Giles, William—buried April 28, 1864, age twenty-eight
Jones, Frances—buried March 13, 1866, age thirteen
Lee, John—buried August 18, 1864, age twenty-one
Lee, Marshall—buried December 30, 1864, age eighteen
Level, infant—buried March 4, 1864, age four months
Level, Joe—buried February 24, 1864, age sixty-five
Lucas, Tom—buried September 25, 1864, age two years and four months
Madden, Belle—buried September 9, 1864, age three
Madden, Betty—buried April 4, 1864, age eight
Madden, infant—buried April 15, 1868, stillborn
Madden, infant—buried February 6, 1866, age three months
Madden, Juliet—buried March 1, 1864, age five
Madden, Mary—buried October 3, 1864, age two years and eight months
Madden, Texia—buried August 9, 1864, age twenty-one
Piper, Abraham—buried February 23, 1864, age three months
Piper, James—buried October 1, 1865, age forty-two

Piper, Williams—buried August 25, 1866, age one and a half years
Ray, John—burial March 11, 1864, age three
Rowe, John—buried August 10, 1865, age six days
Russell, Benjamin—buried August 11, 1864, age fifty-five
Skinner, Celia—buried December 23, 1865, age eleven
Tate, Betsey—buried July 25, 1864, age eighty
Tate, Fountain—buried September 30, 1864, age eight
Tate, James R—buried November 4, 1865, age four
Taylor, Fanny—buried December 8, 1865, age three
Ware, infant—buried January 27, 1867, stillborn
Ware, infant—buried January 4, 1868, no age given

SELECTED SOURCES

Newspapers, Magazines and Registers

Alexandria, Virginia Funeral Programs. On file at the Alexandria Black History Museum.

Alexandria Gazette.

Alexandria Gazette. Obituary section.

Alexandria Gazette Packet.

Alexandria Port Packet.

Baltimore Afro-American. Baltimore, Maryland.

Baltimore Sun.

Hill's Alexandria, Virginia City Directories. Available at the Alexandria Library Local History/Special Collection, 717 Queen Street, Alexandria, Virginia, 22314.

New Journal and Guide. Virginia's oldest weekly African America newspaper, published in Norfolk since 1900.

Vital Statistic Birth Register from 1912–1929. Alexandria Library Local History/Special Collection, 717 Queen Street, Alexandria, Virginia, 22314.

Washington Post and Times-Herald. Washington, D.C.

Washington Times.

Internet Sites

Ancestry.com.

Fold3 Military Records. www.fold3.com.

Marriage and Death Information. www.familysearch.org.
Newspaper Bank. www.genealogybank.com.
The Other Alexandria. https://www.theotheralexandria.com.
Social Security Death Index. www.genealogybank.com.
U.S. Census. https://www.dclibrary.org/heritagequest.
World War I Draft Registration Cards. www.ancestry.com.
World War II Draft Registration Cards. www.ancestry.com.

Personal and Telephone Interviews

Since 2008, more than 510 interviews have been conducted. The individuals here are the ones who connected to the Freedmen's Cemetery.

Joyce Paige Anderson Abney
James P. Alston
Lillian Locklear Alston
Judy Patricia Coles Bailey
Dena Banks
Sherrin Hamilton Bell
Ronald Eugene Burke
Stephanie Burke
Frances Norton Burton
Florence Calloway
Lynnwood Campbell
Lawrence Oliver Carter
Keith Cave
Carol Ann Haskins Daniels
Lois Diggs Davis
Ferdinand T. Day
Richard Diggs
Dana Dishman
Howard Dishman
Bertram D. Drayton
Eugene S. Drayton
Wanda Ellis
Elizabeth Goods Brooks Evans
Charles French
Gwen Day Fuller

Sylvester I. Gaines
Sharon Dunlop Green
Rita Murphy Harris
Gwen Brown Henderson
James E. Henson
Gloria Tancil Holmes
Doris Williams Hughes
Latosha Jackson
Andrew Johnson
Lucian Johnson
Rosalind Drayton Lanford
Bernice Robinson Lee
Yvette Taylor Lewis
James H. Lightfoot
Thelma Dogan Lucas
Irene Gaskins Macklin
ZSun-nee Kimball Miller Matema
Carolyn Phillips McCrae
Mary Morris
Arthur Nelson
Betty Dogan Nicholas
Gale Arlene Brooks Ogden
Lillian Stanton Patterson
Sandy Jordan Porter
Arlette Slaughter Reddick
Fayrene Lyles Richardson
Milton Rowe
Samuel Shanklin
Shirley Sanders Steele
Karen Hubbard Suggs
Herbert P. Tancil
Phyllis Roy Tate
Beatrice Cross Taylor
Dorothy Napper Taylor
John Taylor
Calvin Terrell
Frances Colbert Clements Terrell
Karen Ambush Thande
Eugene R. Thompson

Norma Jennings Turner
Montess Sanders Wales
Clifton Wanzer
Gerald Wanzer
Adrienne Terrell Washington
Paula Haskins Williams

Institutions and Churches

Alexandria, Virginia Courthouse.
Alexandria Black History Museum.
Alexandria Library Local History/Special Collection.
Alfred Street Baptist Church, Alexandria, Virginia.
Arlington, Virginia Courthouse.
Caroline, Virginia Courthouse.
Culpeper, Virginia Courthouse.
Ebenezer Baptist Church, Alexandria, Virginia.
Essex, Virginia Courthouse.
Fairfax, Virginia Courthouse.
Fauquier, Virginia Courthouse.
Frederick, Virginia Courthouse.
Fredericksburg, Virginia Courthouse.
Frederick/Winchester, Virginia Courthouse.
Hanover, Virginia Courthouse.
Henrico, Virginia Courthouse.
King George, Virginia Courthouse.
Library of Virginia, Richmond, Virginia.
Petersburg, Virginia Courthouse.
Prince George, Virginia Courthouse.
Prince William, Virginia Courthouse.
Richmond, Virginia Courthouse.
Roberts Memorial United Methodist Church, Alexandria, Virginia.
Shiloh Baptist Church, Alexandria, Virginia.
Spotsylvania, Virginia Courthouse.
Stafford, Virginia Courthouse.
St. Joseph's Catholic Church, Alexandria, Virginia.
Third Baptist Church, Alexandria, Virginia.
Virginia Historical Society, Richmond, Virginia.

Publications

Miller, T. Michael. *Alexandria & Alexandria (Arlington) County, Virginia: Minister Returns & Marriage Bonds—1801–1852.* Bowie, MD, 1987.

Pippenger, Wesley E. *Alexandria, Virginia—Death Records 1863–1868 and 1869–1896, the Gladwin Record.* Westminster, MD: Willow Bend Books, 2000.

————. *Alexandria, Virginia—Marriages 1870–1892.* Westminster, MD: Family Line Publications, 1994.

————. *Alexandria (Arlington) County, Virginia: Death Records 1853–1896.* Westminster, MD: Family Publications, 1994.

————. *Alexandria County (Arlington), Virginia Marriage Records 1853–1895.* Westminster, MD, 1994.

————. *Tombstone Inscriptions of Alexandria, Virginia.* Vol. 4. Westminster, MD: Family Publications, 1993.

————. *Tombstone Inscriptions of Alexandria, Virginia.* Vol. 3. Westminster, MD: Family Publications, 1992. Revised ed., 1994.

INDEX

ABOUT THE AUTHOR
AND EDITOR

From left to right: Mumini M. Bah, Char McCargo Bah, Maimoona N. Bah Duckenfield and Dwayne Duckenfield.

CHAR MCCARGO BAH is the CEO/owner of FindingThingsforU, LLC. She is a freelance writer for the *Alexandria Gazette*, an independent historian, a professional genealogist, a lecturer and a 2014 Living Legend of Alexandria, Virginia. Char has appeared on numerous television interviews with CBS, FOX-5, Comcast and the Public Broadcasting Service. She is coauthor of *African Americans of Alexandria, Virginia: Beacons of Light in the Twentieth Century.*

MUMINI M. BAH is editor for FindingThingsforU, LLC.